Thomas Lyman Greene

Corporation Finance

a study of the principles and methods of the management of the finances of

corporations in the United States;

Thomas Lyman Greene

Corporation Finance
a study of the principles and methods of the management of the finances of corporations in the United States;

ISBN/EAN: 9783337313128

Printed in Europe, USA, Canada, Australia, Japan

Cover: Foto ©Suzi / pixelio.de

More available books at **www.hansebooks.com**

CORPORATION FINANCE

A STUDY OF THE PRINCIPLES AND METHODS OF THE
MANAGEMENT OF THE FINANCES OF CORPORATIONS
IN THE UNITED STATES ; WITH SPECIAL REFERENCE
TO THE VALUATION OF CORPORATION SECURITIES

BY

THOMAS L. GREENE

AUDITOR, MANHATTAN TRUST COMPANY

G. P. PUTNAM'S SONS

NEW YORK   LONDON
27 WEST TWENTY-THIRD STREET   24 BEDFORD STREET, STRAND

The Knickerbocker Press

1897

The Knickerbocker Press, New York

PREFACE.

BEFORE there can be any intelligent discussion of the problems which arise in the management of corporations, it is necessary that there shall be a wider knowledge of the objects sought in corporation financiering, and of the practical reasons which have led to the policy pursued in the United States, together with its results.

Some suggestions have been made which may, I trust, prove of service to the large class of business men and lawyers who are not infrequently called upon to deal with the incorporation or with the administration of an industrial undertaking ; in the description of the methods of practical finance the attempt has likewise been made to supplement the text-books already in the hands of educators and students.

Experience has developed and brought into prominence business rules and facts which will be useful to an investor in estimating the value of the bonds or shares of corporations in which he may be interested, and it has been the aim to present these rules and practices in such a manner as, while technical in its precision, shall also be available for the purposes of the general reader.

T. L. G.

20 Wall Street, New York City,
    March, 1897.

CONTENTS.

CORPORATION FINANCE

CHAPTER I

BONDS AND STOCKS

THE business man or firm must borrow money. With the few exceptions, where firms have command of practically unlimited sums of their own, business success is possible only through the aid of the money-lender. Let us suppose for illustration that a firm employs a capital of $1,000,000 in its business, one half of which it borrows from the banks on its commercial paper at six per cent. interest. We will suppose also that the firm "turns its capital over" six times a year, which is only another way of saying that its volume of annual sales is six times the capital. Assuming that our firm is enabled to earn two per cent. net upon its sales, the resulting profits, $120,000, amount to twelve per cent. upon the capital employed. As under our assumption the firm is paying six per cent. on the amount borrowed, or $30,000 yearly, it follows that the actual earnings upon the firm's own capital are $90,000, or eighteen per cent., a handsome return made possible only through the borrowing of money which can be used to extend the volume of trade and to earn something for the firm over and above the percentum of interest paid. The actual profits earned under this system vary in different trades, though usually the volume of business is in inverse proportion to the percentage of profit on the annual sales. Whatever sum we select or whatever earnings we assume, the principle underlying the illustration is the same. Of course a part of the capital of such firm or corporation in business must be invested in credits granted to customers and in some form of merchandise in stock.

The practical working out of this fact that borrowing money is now essential to business success, is beneficial to the customer of the firm, to the consumer, and to the people at large. Competition is even more severe between trading firms than in the cases of large manufacturing corporations ; profits tend everywhere to a minimum, so that in the end the percentage of earnings on sales declines toward the level of existence. Slowly, therefore, the possibilities of profit, under this system of doubling or trebling the volume of business through the borrowing of capital, are, through the pressure of competition, taken from the firm and given to the public in the shape of lower prices or superior service. This is the universal law of trade. If we suppose, under our former illustration, that in time the volume of sales reaches eight times the capital employed and that the percentage of profit declines from two per cent. to one per cent., making a return of $80,000 annually, from which as before interest on borrowed capital, amounting to $30,000, is to be deducted, we see that our supposed firm has toiled steadily to increase its trade, has taken large commercial risks in the way of bad debts, declines in the prices of commodities, etc., and has, after all, made but ten per cent. upon its own capital invested and hazarded in its business ; a return too small to compensate for the labor and the danger of loss. Clearly, however, the addition of borrowed capital and the increased volume of trade thereby secured give advantages of profit, in which both firm and customer are entitled to share.

Concurrently with the growth of firms and corporations which do a large business under these conditions, there has come a large increase in the amount of money waiting to be loaned, and a large advance in the methods by which the surplus capital of the world is collected for loaning. Banks, insurance companies, trust companies, and savings banks, in short, firms and corporations, both large and small, formed for every conceivable financial purpose and of every conceivable kind, now stand ready to lend to the deserving borrower. The more depressed the times, the more easily and cheaply can the safe borrower secure needed money. But the greater part of these increasing sums of money is for loan only upon some sort of security. The lenders who are willing to take some risk are few; those who wish to be certain of the return of their money are many. To secure this safety, the owners of this surplus capital are willing to lend it at a low rate of interest. The unwillingness of the average investor, individual or institutional, to put his money at any business hazard, is one of the main causes for the continued fall in the average rate of interest. Capital competes with capital for safe investment.

The demand for security in loans gives the business firm or corporation its opportunity. If perfectly sound in condition and management, it can borrow its outside capital at a low rate, and so increase its own profits. The machinery for gathering money and loaning it has been so perfected, and the knowledge of the conditions of safety in business has become so extended, that the proportion of borrowings to a firm's entire capital has been much increased. Formerly it was with hesitancy that a bank would lend a firm one quarter of its required capital ; now, there is a temptation for a writer to say that a quarter of the firm's own money, with three quarters of borrowings, would be nearer the usual proportion. To borrow one half of one's necessary capital, in money or goods, is common. The comparative ease of obtaining credit, the fall in the average rate of profit made possible by this increase in capital, and the resulting heavy increase in the output and in the volume of trading throughout the world, made necessary in order to earn a fair return under the diminishing ratio of profit, are the forces under which we are witnessing prosperity and depression in almost regular cycles. To take advantage of these trade forces, and at the same time to check the excesses due to them, constitute the great industrial problem of our time.

These conditions of safe lending and mercantile borrowing have drawn a sharp line of distinction in industrial finance. The lenders of money to firms or corporations are creditors, the stockholders are partners in the enterprise. As creditors are willing to furnish capital up to the line of safety, it has become a common saying that the bonds of a corporation ought to cover the minimum value of the property or franchise, leaving the fluctuating or uncertain part of the enterprise to be represented by the shares. This is a good rule, but one which differs in its application to different cases. Loans upon real estate in cities can be made with safety up to a larger percentage of the

appraised value than in towns or upon farms. So too
with corporations or with firms of long standing, whose
style of management is well known, the stability of
whose trade or traffic has been tested by experience,
and where the limits of the expected fluctuations in
volume of commerce can be reasonably predicted ;
such companies or firms can borrow capital up to a
high percentage of their supposed worth. The practical test of this limit of borrowing is found by a consensus of opinion in answer to this question : To what
amount can commercial paper or bonds be floated at
par and at about the ruling rate of interest for such
borrowings ? Even if the firm or company be in exceptionally good credit and able to borrow up to a large
percentage of the real capitalization (including in this
term the guaranties and other fixed charges not
covered by bonds) yet the managers should for their
own future safety conservatively limit their borrowings
to the minimum value of their property as the same
might be estimated in a time of possible adversity.
It is not good financiering to sell evidences of indebtedness at a heavy discount, even though the
stated rate of interest be below the usual percentage.
It is better, if possible, to arrange the rate of interest
so that the bonds or notes will fetch par. It occasionally happens that for sentimental reasons, or perhaps to differentiate a later issue from former ones, a
company will knowingly offend against this rule, and
put out bonds—perhaps under a blanket mortgage-
bearing a low rate of interest for less than their par
value. Since the par value of these bonds must be
paid at maturity, the shareholders, if they wish to protect themselves against the discount, may ask that this
discount be prorated over the number of years to the

maturity of the mortgage and a proportion be deducted from the net earnings each year. The tendency to relieve the present by a sacrifice of the future is natural, but cannot be defended on abstract grounds. For example, a company which might float a five per cent. bond at par chooses to issue a four per cent. bond at (let us say) 80. Of course, to raise a certain amount of money it must then increase the issue by twenty-five per cent. If a million of dollars is needed, the company must put out $1,250,000 of bonds at 80 to obtain the required sum ; the interest to be paid annually meanwhile being the same as though five per cent. bonds had been issued at par. Manifestly, though, such an issue requires the payment of $250,000 extra principal at maturity, an amount which might be pro-rated over the number of years till maturity and deducted each year from income. That would at least serve to remind shareholders of the real expense of such a method of financiering, even when thought to be made necessary by circumstances. The course of the Louisville and Nashville, since 1894, in this very matter deserves commendation. One of the reasons for such issues at a discount is that investors like to buy a bond selling a little less than par, because it offers a better chance for an increase in value than a bond selling at a premium. If it requires a rate of interest far above the ruling market rate to enable the issue to fetch par, it is a proof that the amount of principal asked for is too large for the business to support.

· To issue bonds or commercial paper at too high a rate of interest or at too great a discount from the face value, except for special reasons, is a violation of the principle upon which modern industrial debt financiering is based. As we have seen, this principle is that as large a part of the required capital must be borrowed at as low a rate of interest as will enable the partners in the enterprise to use those borrowings in their business with safety and at a profit to themselves. If the partners or shareholders of a new enterprise are not willing to contribute the necessary money beyond this secure proportion, there is something doubtful about the outcome. What has been said about firms applies with changed circumstances and names to corporations. They, too, must borrow, though their borrowings may take the form of a mortgage rather than that of commercial paper. We occasionally read of a surface railway or other company which has no bonds upon its property, but only shares. If the enterprise is at the beginning so doubtful that borrowed money would endanger success, the promoters do well to take all the risk, providing they have faith in the outcome. But in the case of a corporation starting with something assured, or where experience has demonstrated that there is a margin of safety, to avoid borrowing may not be good financiering. A street electric railway paying six per cent. on its stock could sell bonds up to half of its capital on a basis, we will say, of five per cent. interest. By issuing such bonds it could, on the same earnings, pay seven per cent. instead of six per cent. on its capital stock. Every profitable corporation, if it so decides, may rightly take all the advantage possible of these principles in the management of its finances.

The shareholders in a corporation are the partners; they take the risks of the business, and are not only entitled to all profits but may rightly increase those profits by every legitimate means. It is also a business question whether the share capital should be subdivided into classes with a preference of one class over another. In the cases of certain trading or manufacturing companies no bonds are issued, the capital being divided into one or more classes of preferred shares together with common stock. The corporation of H. B. Claflin Company in New York City is an instance in point. This company was formed in 1890 to take over the dry-goods jobbing business of H. B. Claflin & Co. It has a capital of $9,000,000, divided into first preferred stock, bearing cumulative dividends of five per cent., second preferred stock, bearing cumulative dividends of six per cent., and common shares covering nearly one half of the capitalization. In such cases the higher shares should have the preference not only in dividends, but in claims upon the assets ; in return for which privilege they are limited to a certain but comparatively small rate of dividend annually. Such shares usually carry a cumulative claim as against the other classes, which means that a dividend passed at any one quarter or year must be made up from future earnings before the lower shares receive any return. Under such circumstances these preference stocks really take the place of bonds, and are to be so considered in theory. Their advantage over bonds lies in this, that in years of extreme depression or of great trade losses, suspension of preference payments does not involve foreclosure and loss to the common stock, because time is allowed in which to make up such losses. In the cases of corporations formed to take over trading or manufacturing concerns in whose business violent fluctuations are possible, the issue of preference stocks instead of bonds is to be commended ; but with companies whose business may reasonably be called stable, bonds are in better favor. In both instances much depends upon the management, but the average investor seems to think himself more secure where annual payments of interest are obligatory ; he believes that a little pressure upon the management has often a good effect.

In the United States the majority of preference shares in the hands of the public represent equitable claims upon future or present prosperity. They were generally issued by the railways as evidences of debt which the exigencies of the times required should be deferred ; perhaps some peculiar obligation not then easily paid ; but more probably, such preferred shares were given to old bondholders who were compelled by insolvency to yield something of the principal and interest of their then debt. In 1888 the Chesapeake and Ohio Railway was reorganized without foreclosure, the bondholders consenting to readjust their claims. The " B " bonds of the old company (bearing six per cent.), dated 1878, were exchanged for two thirds of their face value into new five per cent. bonds, and for one third into first preferred stock. The company becoming more prosperous, this first preferred stock was, in 1893, exchanged two thirds into " blanket " four and a half per cent. bonds, and one third into common stock. This process relieved the needs of the company at the time, while afterwards the holders of old " B " bonds received more than the value of their original investment.

The Lake Superior and Mississippi Railroad was sold under foreclosure in 1877 to the holders of its first mortgage bonds, who exchanged their bonds into preferred shares at the rate of $1200 of such shares for each bond of $1000. The new company, the St. Paul and Duluth, thereupon issued a new first mortgage, bearing five per cent. In time a second mortgage was put upon the property for extensions and improvements. Under this policy the necessities of the situation were met, and after 1883 the course of the old first mortgage holders was justified by the receipt of regular dividends upon the preferred shares ; without such concession the loss to such holders would have no doubt been almost total.

Though no stronger for these reasons legally, preference stocks issued to represent deferred claims embody an ethically good claim upon the general or future prosperity.

At other times companies having only common shares may like to exchange a part in certain proportions for preferred. In such cases the motive is often sentimental ; the company may be earning a small sum over fixed charges (bond interest, rentals, and taxes), a sum too small for division among a large number of common shares, but enough to pay, perhaps, four per cent. on a small preferred capital. It is considered better to pay that four per cent. if the capital is arranged so as to allow of it, because such payment, or, in fact, any honest payment of dividends, improves the credit of the company in the eyes of the public. Sentiment is an important factor in corporation financiering, one of which the good manager will make legitimate use. It is, however, an abuse of sentiment where dividends not fairly earned are paid in order that the credit of the corporation may have a fictitious support. The declaration of dividends on the preference bonds of the Philadelphia and Reading in 1893, followed a month later by the bankruptcy of the company and the placing of the property in the hands of receivers, is open to the above criticism. An exception to this statement should be made in cases where a succession of prosperous years is followed by a period of losses ; if recovery

seems fairly in sight, it is proper to continue such dividend payments for a while rather than destroy the continuity of such returns to shareholders. An instance is
that of the Chicago, Burlington, and Quincy, a company
which suffered severe losses, in 1888, through a strike
among its enginemen. Though confessedly not having
earned it, the company paid the dividend, and was
under the circumstances justified in so doing. The
statements made regarding the stocks and bonds of
railway companies are true also as to the bonds and
stocks of other corporations, though changes must be
made to meet the circumstances of each case.

In instances where large corporations have been
formed for the prosecution of enterprises which demand
large plants and extensive organizations for the carrying on of the business, the same remarks may be made
without much modification. Such extensive companies
formed, say, for the manufacture of certain particular
articles in much demand, require the expenditure of
large sums of money for special machinery and for the
erection of buildings specially designed for the purpose
of the business. This plant and machinery may be
almost valueless for any other purpose than for this
particular manufacture. Bonds issued by such a company are, like railway mortgages, really dependent
upon the success of the corporation and its business,
since usually the amount of such bonds is largely in
excess of the value of the land and machinery if sold
for any other than the original purpose of manu
facturing. The difference between the valuation of
the plant at forced sale and the amount for which it is
bonded, represents the good will of the business, whether
it is so stated in the company's accounts or not. It
does not alter the case to say that the amount of the

bonded indebtedness (or preferred stock) has really been expended by the company upon its property. The lien is not so much upon the property itself as upon the business success of the company. Yet that success may be so reasonably sure that it may properly form the basis for borrowing at a low rate of interest. Those who have knowledge of the particular line of manufacturing which the new company is to pursue, may be clear in their judgment that the success of the company will be beyond a peradventure. Yet for the investor or for the banks or for the capitalist generally, nothing can take the place of experience as the basis of a judgment as to corporation values. When a company has been running long enough to enable the ordinary lender of money to form such a judgment, he is usually willing to grant the company a larger proportion of credit than was at first obtainable.

The fact, however, that at first only a comparatively small proportion of the required capital could be borrowed at ordinary rates of interest may have led the promoters of such enterprises to try to borrow a still larger sum, with the result that the extra risk as estimated by the banking houses is paid for during the whole life of the bonds by an unusually high rate of interest, or, which is the same thing, by a heavy discount from the par value of the bonds issued. An instance of such a discount is afforded by a prominent railroad company. This company issued ten-forty adjustment bonds, bearing six per cent. These bonds were so named because they could be called in by the company at 110 and cancelled ten years from date, becoming due in forty years. These bonds, after first being offered to the shareholders, were sold at 57½ with a bonus of stock at 22½. In other words, for $800 in cash the purchaser received one $1000 adjustment bond and $1000 in stock at par. Thus the bonds practically cost the purchaser about $350 each. The then managers, representing foreign stockholders, finding the company pressed for ready money to take up called loans (temporarily, as it turned out), thought themselves compelled to offer such severe terms ; the situation having become acute through mistakes in financial policy in previous years. The credit of the company having meanwhile greatly improved, these bonds were paid in 10 years. The conversion of the Atchison incomes into " A " and " B " bonds in 1892 is an illustration of the mortgaging of future prosperity to relieve present needs for money. Such extra interest or discount is a measure of the badness of the financiering or of the pressure of necessity, and in times of depression may even cause such a financial pressure of annual charges as in effect to be a reason for bankruptcy. When we hear it stated, as we sometimes do, that a particular business cannot bear the high rates of interest which it is directly or indirectly paying, we may rightly assume, in the absence of some other oppressing cause, that the reason for the present distress goes back to the time when the promoters of the enterprise or the organizers of the newly incorporated company formed to take over an old business, were unwilling to accept the estimate of experienced money-lenders upon the success of the company. Either by advancing their own money or by inducing others to become partners in the enterprise, they ought to have obtained share capital enough so as to have started the enterprise conservatively ; one important element of this conservatism being that only so much money should be borrowed as could be obtained on favorable terms.

In the cases of comparatively small corporations formed for trading purposes or to prosecute a business comparatively small in volume, care must be exercised by both organizers and lenders of money. The bonds of such corporations are not eagerly sought for from the nature of the case. Sometimes, as has been already remarked, the financiering of such corporations is accomplished by the issuing of preferred stocks instead of bonds. So far as the general public is concerned, the borrowing of money on the part of such small companies does not differ greatly from the procedure observed in the borrowing of money on commercial paper by partners. But few of the bonds of these small companies reach the public ; the principal source of supply for borrowings being the banks. The banks in lending money to these small corporations require statements from them the same as in the cases of firms ; but because of the difference in responsibility between partners and corporations, lending institutions, in addition to the claim upon the assets of the company, usually demand the personal endorsement of the officers, thus in effect securing from such small companies the personal liability of the managers precisely as though the business were the property of an individual or a firm.

Municipal bonds form an exception to the rules of borrowing according to the probability of successful business. A municipality is any territorial subdivision of a country, city, county, village, or township, which may wish to borrow money for any improvement allowed by law. The security for such borrowings does not rest primarily upon business profits but upon the property embraced, though in the long run property valuations in any city or county must depend upon the prosperity

of the community. Usually the power to bond the
town is limited by law to an amount covering so small
a percentage of the town values that the question of
the security of such bonds, from the point of view of
the sufficiency of the property pledged, does not often
arise.

On this account municipal bonds, when they are
good, are very good indeed, and command high prices
at the hands of a special class of investors, such as savings banks and insurance companies. The dangers of
municipal bonds arise from another quarter. The questions of legality of issue are so complex, and, as even
after able legal opinions, unexpected difficulties may be
encountered, their purchase becomes a matter of some
risk, including perhaps a long-contested lawsuit, in
cases where counties and towns may for any reason
desire to repudiate their obligations. For these reasons,
cities enjoying good credit can sell their bonds at the
lowest rate of interest known in financial circles ; while
as for the bonds of other less known municipal divis-
ions, only such institutions as have unlimited resources
for investigation and for the enforcement of the payment, if found necessary, become the purchasers. In
general, municipal bonds are not favorite forms of investment with the average capitalist.

CHAPTER II

FORMS OF CORPORATE ENTERPRISE

WHEN a firm, established long enough to give its returns some stability, desires to sell its business, it soon finds that the easiest way to accomplish this result is by incorporation. When the company is decided upon or formed, the bonds or shares become available for public sale or subscription in any desired amounts. In this way a large business with its plant can be sold by piecemeal, as it were, at a total valuation which could not be obtained in any other way. The larger the business the more difficult is it to find partnership purchasers.

The usual course in such matters is to consult some banking or promoting house which can be induced to finance the project (*i. e.*, to furnish any money required during the transfer), and which has facilities for disposing of the new bonds or shares to its customers and the public. It is a tendency of the times to give the sale of public securities into the hands of those whose profession is that of judging of the values of the securities to be offered. The majority of the investors have their own concerns to look after, and in any case are not good judges of bonds or shares or of the prospects of success of special enterprises. Such persons in the end take the advice of trusted banking houses. Since the reputation of such houses is very important to them, they take pains not to recommend purchases which may involve their customers in losses. Conversely their recommendation is much sought after for new enterprises, and to pay their charges is the cheapest way in the long run to " float " a public corporation. These remarks, of course, do not apply to cases where all of the new capital is retained by the old partners.

Where such houses are consulted by the would-be incorporators there is usually a difference as to the value to be put upon the enterprise ; the owners are perhaps over-sanguine; the banking house, if conservative, goes through the submitted facts and figures in cold blood. It knows, too, approximately, what the public will be willing to pay. The capitalization is then fixed at a sum which it is supposed will allow of a small distribution of profits even in poor years.

There is first the division of the capital into bonds (or preferred stock) and common shares. In order that money may be borrowed at the lowest rate of interest, and thus every possible profit be reserved for the common stock, it is necessary that bonds should be issued only to the minimum value of the property. When preferred stock has a preference not only as to dividends but also as to assets in cases of failure, it takes the place of bonds and should be regarded in the light of a debt. What this minimum value is, is not an easy question to determine. Sometimes it is taken to include the values of the buildings, machinery (or other contents), and the raw material on hand or in process of manufacture. Whether this is safe depends in part upon the nature of the business. Sometimes real-estate experts are asked to appraise the plant as a basis for bonds ; but here care should be taken as to

2

the instructions given to such appraisers. If they are required to give an opinion on the value of the ground, buildings, etc., for the use of that particular business, they may honestly put their appraisal at figures far above anything which could be obtained at forced sale in case of insolvency, and security in such an event is the very thing sought for by the bondholder. In the same way and under similar instructions an extravagant valuation may be put upon the machinery, which may not be new, and indeed may already be in process of supersedure as to kind in other and competing establishments. The raw or half-worked up material should be also computed at prices which allow for possible fluctuations because of changes in fashions or by reason of any circumstances which may affect the particular business under consideration. Yet bonds aggregating a larger sum than the valuation of the plant at forced sale may be legitimate and safe because of the stable nature of the manufacturing or trading to be taken over by the new company. But in such cases it should be distinctly understood that a part of such bonded debt rests for security upon success rather than upon real-estate values, *i. e.*, upon the " good-will."

The amount of common stock to be issued does not occasion so much trouble. Allowing for the ups and downs of business, the common capital should fairly represent the fluctuating possibilities of the new concern. To estimate this future properly, the number of common shares should be conservatively small ; but the difficulty here, as everywhere else in corporation financiering, is the dislike of the public to the payment by a corporation of dividends higher than the normal rate of interest. It is better financiering to pay good returns in good years, thus allowing for a decline in periods of depression, than to capitalize the company up to the highest point with the possible result of making the whole common issue of little or no value in poor years —and worthless shares are always a menace to honest business.

In asking for subscriptions to bonds or shares in a new corporation formed to take over a manufacturing or trading business, it is usual to employ reputable public accountants who are required to make a report stating what the profits have been for a number of years. These accountants' certificates have had great weight with purchasers, but recent events have limited their importance. Too much meaning was found in such certificates by small capitalists ; they were construed practically to guarantee the whole corporation and its future. As a matter of fact, those certificates were valuable as giving an expert statement of the books of the old partnership as they stood ; but they were not intended to explain or to sit in judgment upon the commercial facts which lay behind those books. Being employed by the old partnership or by the promoting house, such accountants may have examined only such accounts as they were requested to, made statements in the form desired, or omitted items which they were not paid to investigate. A firm of account- ants might certify that the average annual profits for three years were a given sum, and stop their report at that point. If the partners had a year previously formed the resolution to incorporate, they might easily swell their revenues greatly during the last year. The discrepancy would be detected if the earnings were given for each year separately, but not if an average alone were stated. Again, the form of such a certificate might be that the accounts and bills receivable exceeded those payable by a given sum which might be added to the assets to be covered by the proposed share capital ; and such a statement, while true, might be misleading. The accounts receivable might be such as were always outstanding, for which working capital should be provided in the plan of capitalization. If so, and every business needs more or less of such working sums of money, simply to offset them by bills payable —meaning money borrowed from the banks—is, under the circumstances, manifestly improper. Borrowed money is a debt, and the plan of incorporation under discussion assumes that the bonds or preferred stock covers the whole of that debt. This particular error in incorporating is sometimes ventured upon in order to give to the old partners all the money subscribed by the public for the bonds and common stock, but it conceals the real status of the finances and leaves unguarded a possible danger. Moreover, bills payable must be met in full while the running accounts of customers may not be worth their face, leaving a deficiency not covered by such a plan of incorporation. The rise and fall of the Thurber-Whyland Company in New York City furnishes an example.

It may be that the certificate unintentionally misleads in another way. The books may be exact in giving the earnings and expenses for the previous year, and yet the resulting profits may not be a proper basis for corporate capitalization ; for the reason that selling prices may have been exceptionally high or the cost of raw material or of some important item of expense exceptionally low, so that the year's profits may be too good for an estimate of the future. The case of the Allsopp Brewery in England is an illustration. For these reasons, the course for those proposing to incorporate themselves, or to promote such incorporation, or to purchase the bonds and shares in the new company, is to supplement the information furnished by the accountant with other expert knowledge regarding the circumstances and conditions under which the particular business has been and is likely to be carried on.

A matter which should be considered is that of management. Practiced experience, as well as the best economic theory, lays emphasis upon the importance of an able manager. Nothing can take his place ; and his rewards in the shape of salary or returns upon his shares, must be commensurate with his importance. In building up a business the personal element is a great factor. In railways there has been developed in the process of time a body of specialists who are trained in their work of superintending and managing railroad operations, and from whom men may always be had by any company to take control. This same thing will in time be true of all corporation work which concerns the production or distribution of staple goods or necessaries, and, indeed, this is true already of certain lines of work ; but it is a point to be considered by all interested in new corporations whether expert management can be had, particularly if those who brought the old firm up to its place of importance are soon to drop out of control through age or lack of interest. When our important corporations have passed their experimental stage, proper management will be largely a question of proper payment.

Aside from the advantages which the corporate form offers for the gathering of capital in small sums for some great enterprise, for the massing of men and machinery at some proper spot, and for the conduct of

a large business at a small expense per unit of output,
there are benefits to other and smaller concerns by the
transfer into corporations.   It often happens that partnerships are turned into companies without intention
to become public concerns.   Perhaps a number of persons acquire an interest in a business established and
built up by a father and uncle, a business which it is
intended to keep in the family.   But the multiplication
of owners occasions much difficulty, while another
death or two may put the whole enterprise in peril,
perhaps require a selling out to other parties in order
to determine the value which would then require to be
divided.   These perils lying in the path of firms having many partners, some minors, some women, are well
understood.   Some of them may be guarded against by
such devices as insuring the lives of the managing partners ; but many of such instances are best solved by
organizing a corporation to carry on the business ; in
this way the proportion of each partner or heir can be
set aside in shares, which can be transferred or sold in
any proportion or at any price without affecting the
business itself.   Nor will death destroy the living of
the remaining owners ; for corporations do not die with
the death of shareholders.   One of the arguments
against trading coporations is that the new company
may lose the advantage of the zeal and ability of the
manager who has brought the business up to its present
state of profitableness, but who having now no such
interest in the result will drop out altogether, or will
not give it the old and close attention.   In scattered
instances this may be a good objection, for we should
not omit the personal equation from our calculations.
To supply a class of managing specialists in trading or
manufacturing is a work of time ; but if a particular

line of trading or manufacturing is large enough to demand expert management and to give remunerative employment to those who will study the business, such a class will surely arise to meet that demand. The only danger is that until a good manager is born and made, the business may suffer to a certain extent. It is proper to take the contingency into account in estimating on the probable future values of the bonds and shares of a corporation if offered for public subscription or sale. In some cases the contingency may be provided for by arranging to have the old managers retain a large interest for a certain number of years, or in any way which will make future success an advantage to the old partners.

But to partners who form a company for family reasons, these possible objections do not apply. The status of such companies is directly affected by the fact that no bonds or shares are to be sold to the public ; therefore the public are concerned with the success or failure of such a family company only so far as that company may wish to borrow money from the banks or ask for credit on goods purchased. In such cases equity requires a complete exhibit of their affairs to those who have a right to that information. For the public at large, and for the information of the state which granted the charter of incorporation, a statement of the assets and liabilities in brief form is properly demanded. The profits of a family company is not a matter with which the state need concern itself. The limits of liability under a corporate form are well understood, and if liability is limited, so also is the credit ; no undue advantage is taken of anybody by incorporation. Bank officers when asked for loans will either accept the signature of the company through its proper representative, or will demand the personal endorsement of some individuals; the matter of credit in family corporations regulates itself.

A defect in our general laws touching corporations is often the neglect to distinguish between those companies which are public in their nature and those which are private. A company whose bonds or shares are held by the public and which depends upon public support for its financiering, ought to be compelled (if it does not agree of its own motion) to give out its business accounts in such detail that the holders of its bonds or preferred or common stocks can form a clear idea of the profitableness, of the financial standing, and of the managerial success of their company. But private or family companies are under no obligations to the public as to their affairs except as already noted, and should not be required to make returns in detail. The distinction between public and private corporations would at times be difficult to draw; no rule could be made which would not sometimes err. Perhaps a limit to the number of stockholders would furnish a practical test under which such a distinction could be made.

It is sometimes thought that the legal restrictions imposed upon corporations and the state oversight to which they are subjected, are such drawbacks to the corporate form as to balance the advantages already referred to. Such restriction and such oversight will probably never be withdrawn; indeed, the tendency of the times—as evidenced as much in economic discussion as in actual legislation—is toward further restraint. The matter of stock or bond watering often has business effects which a prolonged strike or some other commercial event can alone make clear; the whole discussion as to "monopoly," though somewhat crude as yet, may, as regards future legislation, turn in the end upon the question whether the profits arising from combination or from huge corporations have been equitably divided between the three parties in interest : the company itself, the consuming public, and the employees. To answer such a question, the widest information will be necessary. Corporations, therefore, should not look forward to any general reduction in the amount of state regulation.

But while this seems to be true generally, it by no means follows that corporations will find that form of doing business less favorable than before. If we keep in mind the fact that a corporation—a public company —implies a well-established business on a scale so great as to require large capital and a large and well equipped plant, it will be seen that the best success cannot come from the partnership form. If we accept a large output or traffic and a correspondingly low cost per unit of production as the criterion of a well-managed company, we necessarily imply a large business enjoying good credit and with years of experience behind it, things which are not so hopefully to be expected from a firm. Such a company must, in the nature of the case, have an element in its business which, from want of a better word, may be called monopolistic ; if that advantage is used for the public good there should be no complaint ; it is an advantage in the hands of a skilful manager for which the company may well pay by giving publicity to its affairs. Nor should it be forgotten that in such cases publicity does not have the drawbacks urged by small trading companies that it invites competition. If our supposed company is well managed and is doing business at a low ratio of profit, publication of its affairs rather repels competition by showing the hopelessness of success to a new company.

Precisely because a large volume of transporting or manufacturing is essential to the stability and long-continued success of an ideal corporation, so such corporations tend gradually to absorb the production of such articles as can be carried or manufactured in large quantities, and, of course, consumed by the public in like amounts. Generally such articles are the necessaries of life, or if not strictly speaking necessaries, then those with which the consuming public are especially concerned. From this point of view also we must expect in the future additional legislation. The best defence of corporations against unduly severe laws is full publicity. The history of a company, its early losses and struggles, the prices of the commodity when the business was begun compared with prices now, the cost of production per pound or gallon or barrel, showing the reduction, and in view of such facts the moderate profits of to-day—statements such as these will prove to be the best defence against drastic legislation before the bar of public opinion. But a company relying upon such a defence must be sure that its course as regards prices and policy is one which cannot be fairly attacked. For these reasons, while the restrictions imposed by the state are sometimes onerous and often foolish, yet the advantages of the corporate form for the prosecution of a large and stable business must outweigh the disadvantages. Probably the question of taxation is a serious one for most corporations. Their form and their business seem to invite taxation. It may be that for a time corporations will be obliged to carry more than their proportionate share of the common burden in this respect. In the end this question will run into the more general one of the rightful profits to be made; but meanwhile taxes are things for which incorporations must be prepared.

Corporations formed to carry on a business semi-public in its nature, like that of supplying water and gas to the citizens of cities and towns, do not need extended discussion. So far as the arrangement of their finances is concerned, it should not depart greatly from the principles already laid down for the formation of manufacturing companies. Into the matter of governmental ownership it is not purposed to enter here ; but regarded from the financial point of view the amount of bonded indebtedness should not exceed the safe value of the property conservatively estimated. Gas and water companies do not indeed often offend in these particulars, since in successful cases the shares have so increased in value as to leave no doubt of the conservatism of the original financial plan. The investor should look into the probability of losses by reason of a change in policy on the part of the community, or because of the beginning of the enterprise on a scale of expenditure not warranted by the probabilities. Yet water and gas are modern necessaries of life, and the supplying of these necessaries, when done by private companies under a conservative plan, is a proper and safe business for the investment of money.

Another form of industrial enterprise destined to assume an important position in investment finance, is that of supplying street transportation to the inhabitants of cities and towns. The rapid growth in the use of electrical power has carried the matter of surface railways in and between cities and villages to a position of great importance. As forming the basis for the

investment of capital there can be nothing better than
the street traffic of our cities.   Experience has demonstrated that such traffic is even more constant and
stable than that of steam railroads, and is capable of
yet greater development, as surface car lines are extended to meet the demands of a spreading population
and as travel increases in proportion as the facilities
of easy and rapid transit are increased.

But while the safety of street travel as a basis for
the investment of capital cannot be disputed, there
may remain questions about the values of the bonds
and shares of individual street railway companies for
whose settlement further time is required.   Some six
or eight years ago the motive power of street lines
was the horse ; but electricity, it was soon found,
upset all the old calculations of receipts and expenses.
The capitalization of the company was increased by
the cost of the new power but so was the volume of
travel, so that great profits were shown to have been
earned.

The demand for electric equipment led to its manufacture in such quantities and under such uniformity
of detail that the prices of new motors and the like fell
to one half the old figures.   Study and experience
found ways of keeping rolling stock and motors in
repair at a cost formerly believed impossible ; and
meanwhile the traffic receipts continued to increase
steadily and regularly as the public came to realize
the improvements in street conveyance and to take
increasing advantage of them.

In the cases of companies freshly established and
operating in large cities, it may be assumed, for the purposes of a rough calculation, that the roadbed will re-

quire a complete renewal in ten or twelve years, the overhead construction (if the trolley is used) within fifteen years, the electric station and buildings in from twenty-five to fifty years, the car bodies in twelve or fifteen years, and the motor trucks in ten or twelve years, with the steam machinery in fifteen years. These averages of life should, of course, be extended in cases where circumstances would make such a test too severe, as, for instance, in interurban lines using the turnpikes. When, however, fair averages can be obtained and the cost of such renewals estimated, it will be possible for those interested in a new road to make a hypothetical calculation of the average annual earnings for the future, leaving the expected increase in traffic as an offset to any possible error in the calculation.

We are now accumulating a mass of experiences and figures about street railway companies which will place the bonds and shares of those companies on as sure a basis as those of steam railroads and as fully entitled to the good opinion of the investing public. Meanwhile, an approximate result can be obtained by any one who will take the time and trouble to make a thorough analysis of the condition and circumstances in any particular case.

A matter to be considered also is the life of the charters of the street companies and the rights to the use of the highway. Generally speaking, the American public are not disposed to be unfair, and a practical seizure of street railway property by a forfeiture of the charter or by a refusal to renew the same without compensation is not to be expected. On the other hand, it is often a matter of importance how far the company is protected against competition perhaps on adjoining streets. It is well also to examine the provisions of the charter to see whether they contain requirements which may prove onerous in the future.

Throughout this book the form of corporation discussed is that of the company whose capitalization rests directly upon the property, and whose shares are owned by individuals. There is, however, a company of another sort formed under the laws of certain States, particularly New Jersey, which permit corporations to hold the shares of other corporations. In such instances the company does not itself hold property or manage a business, but issues its bonds or shares upon the bonds or shares of other and operating companies held in its treasury; it is, in short, a corporation of corporations.

In certain lines of business such financing companies are the logical result of the movement toward consolidation, of which the simple company was the first outcome. In some cases no other method of concentration seems possible. Perhaps the production of some article requires that the various processes shall be conducted in as many different States whose laws demand that the business within that State shall be conducted by a company incorporated by that State. If all these subsidiary companies are to work in harmony there must be some method of uniform management, brought about most easily by a common ownership of the different shares. Economically speaking, such financing companies are to be judged by their results, precisely as in the case of simple corporations.

Companies are sometimes formed to hold the shares of other companies, principally to prevent competition and to stop the reduction in prices that perhaps previously to such common ownership was bringing disaster

upon all concerned. Financial insolvency is a thing to
be dreaded for its own sake ; and when it would apparently lead to no better conditions than before, it con-
fers no benefit upon the community. Such companies
are, as before, judged by their ultimate results, society
at large being adverse to such combinations only as
they may prevent genuine progress through the formation of still larger single companies able to reduce costs
to themselves and prices to the consumer. Such combinations are sometimes made through Trust agreements, which purport to give to the old proprietors in
lieu of their old title, a trustee's certificate stating that
they are entitled to such a proportion in the equity of
all the combined businesses as their original property
bore to the whole, these various values being previously fixed by negotiations between those concerned.
The public at large are hostile to such Trusts, believing
them to be secret agreements in restraint of trade and
against the interests of the community. Moreover,
they appear to be unnecessary, since all the essential
advantages of a Trust can be secured under the form
of a lawful corporation either simple or compound.

Where the properties sought to be combined have
been owned by firms or individuals, it has often been
found expedient to transfer the title of such properties,
perhaps lying in different States, directly to the combining company in return for the issue of bonds and
shares of the new company in agreed proportions. In
such cases the possible advantages are that it may give
to the new company the knowledge and skill possessed
in different degrees and about different parts of the process by the old proprietors, for common use ; that it
may prevent frauds in weight and quality which the
previous extreme competition may have brought about ;

and that it may allow a concentration of buying and selling at the least expense and with better results. If a reasonable share of these advantages is given to the public in one form or another, the new company has a strong argument for its existence.

As to the finances of such huge corporations, or of companies holding the shares of other companies, they do not differ in principle from the rules already quoted regarding simple corporations. The bonds issued (including the underlying liens, if any) should not exceed in amount the minimum worth of the property, and the shares should fairly represent the fluctuating values remaining. The bonds and shares of such great combining corporations, generally speaking, are not quoted on the exchanges at as high a range as those of railways. This may be due partly to the fact that the business of the company may be, from the nature of the case, highly speculative in character, and therefore uncertain as to results in any particular year ; or its affairs may be in the hands of men perhaps experienced in that particular line of business, but who have not yet acquired a reputation with the investing public ; or perhaps there may be on its board of directors or among its officers no one in whom capitalists have confidence as experienced in financial management, for the department of the finances in corporation affairs requires special care and ability just as does the manufacturing or trading. Time will be required to bring about a settled public opinion as to the degree of value which can safely be put upon the businesses of huge industrial combinations or corporations.

CHAPTER III

WHEN the owner of a dwelling-house executes a mortgage upon his property up to a certain percentage of its assumed value, the transaction, so far as the financiering is concerned, is not different in theory from similar transactions when entered into on a larger scale by corporations. The lender of the money first inquires into the safety of his loan. He does not wish to become in effect a partner with the mortgageor by making himself dependent even to a small extent upon the success of the borrower in business. He loans the borrower a sum of money equal to one half or two thirds of the appraised value of the dwelling-house, considering this proportion of that value as secure even under a forced sale. Practically, therefore, the mortgageor, as in the case of corporations, borrows money at a comparatively low rate of interest upon the minimum value of his property. If the sum asked for is in excess of these percentages of the value the loan is refused, or if accepted is taken at a correspondingly high rate of interest, thus violating the principle of debt financiering already discussed.

Mortgages upon dwelling-houses differ, however, in some important points from the debts due by corporations. The lender of money upon ordinary real estate does not rely for security upon the success of the bor-

3

rower in business,—that has already been stated ; but neither does the lender rely upon the profitableness of the profession or trade in which the mortgageor is engaged. The reliance is rather upon the business success of all citizens, with allowances, of course, for advances or reductions in values of real estate which may come from the shiftings of population or the caprices of fashion. If the mortgageor should be unable to pay the interest on his mortgage when due, and the property should be offered for sale under foreclosure proceedings, any man in any line of business may become the purchaser. In short, the property and its value is not dependent upon any one man or any one trade, but upon the prosperity of the whole community.

This is not generally the case with large corporations. The railway lines in the United States, for example, vary in cost from $15,000 to $200,000 per mile, with an average of about $50,000. They are bonded for an average of $32,000 per mile. Railway lines are expensive to construct. A roadbed must be built up and made fit to bear the running of trains ; the erection of costly bridges and other works must be undertaken ; rails and ties must be bought, so that the railroad properties as they exist to-day could not be duplicated for the amount of their bonded debt ; yet if the trains were to stop running, the rails and ties would be worthless except for old iron and wood, while the right of way could be sold to the neighboring farmers only at a low valuation per acre. The whole property of a railroad company, considered simply as real estate and old material, is worth but a small fraction of the amount for which it is mortgaged. The creditors of the company depend for the security of their money not upon the property considered as such, but upon the business for which the company was organized ; that is, upon the transportation of passengers and goods. If that transportation yields a profit, the bonds are safe, otherwise not. The bondholders cannot, as in the case of a dwelling-house, hope to sell the property to any companies except those engaged in transportation. The American law and the wording of American railway mortgages state the lien to be upon the property ; but, commercially speaking, this is not correct ; the mortgage is really upon the company's revenues. But railway trains must continue to be run. Not only is there a public duty involved which forbids the State to allow the stoppage of railway working except in extreme cases, but, since the value of the bonds depends upon income, the operations which produce that income must be continued even though the result be in part unfavorable ; otherwise the loss would be total. But since railways must be worked, the expenses of working must be paid. Sufficient material and supplies must be bought, the claims of employees for wages must be met, and everything reasonably necessary for the proper operation of the railway must be paid from current revenues. It is seen, therefore, that the lien of a railway bond is finally shifted from the real estate to the gross earnings and then to the net earnings of the company.

The statement that the real lien of a railway bond is upon the commercial success of the company as a carrier of traffic explains some of the anomalies of corporation practice. The railway mortgage repeats in the strongest legal phrases the supposed fact that, if interest or principal is not paid when due, or if any other provision is not complied with, then the mortgage shall be foreclosed and the property sold to the highest bidder.

This is a legal fiction. Although the terms are the same in railway mortgages as in those on dwelling-houses, the commercial facts just mentioned forbid compliance with them. In the great majority of cases the selling of a railway at forced sale, even to another company, is out of the question except as the result of reorganization. Partly to give the appearance of living up to the terms of the mortgage and partly to prevent those terms from being literally carried out, the courts appoint receivers for railway properties in bankruptcy or about to become so. Out of this contradiction between the too strong language of our railway mortgages and the commercial facts which control, has arisen the American custom of appointing railway receivers, a custom which is in the course of evolution, both as to the law and as to the practice under that law. The English " debenture " expresses the real situation more clearly than the American bond. The former by its language limits its lien to the earning capacity of the company, though the real liens are the same in both cases. Probably the American custom of putting into the railway mortgage terms which are stronger than the commercial facts warrant was due to the feeling, at one time prevalent, that the granting by the company of a number of legal rights (such as foreclosure) supposed to be absolute, added to the value of the security. Something of this feeling remains with us yet, for in the United States the debenture bond, except when issued by companies of unusual credit, like the New York Central, is not classed as high as bonds drawn in the American fashion.

The principal use of the right of foreclosure in railway bonds is to convey title to a reorganization committee in case of insolvency. The courts are always

careful to insist upon the carrying out of the forms and
remedies provided for in the mortgage, when cases of
this sort are brought before them. Yet so well understood is the real situation that the same courts will ask
the creditors of a bankrupt company to be speedy in
coming to some agreement in order that the receivers
may be discharged ; implying that the receivers are
operating the property in order to keep the road running and to prevent disintegration of the system as a
temporary expedient, until some readjustment of the
obligations can be made ; and such indeed is the actual
practice. The Richmond and West Point Terminal
Railway and Warehouse Company, a financing corporation formed to control other companies, became bankrupt
in 1892. An elaborate plan of reorganization embrac-
ing the subsidiary companies was promulgated in 1894
under the name of the Southern Railway Company.
To bring the different properties under one company,
foreclosure proceedings were begun and carried out
against the Richmond and Danville Railroad Company,
under its consolidated mortgage of 1886, and against
the East Tennessee, Virginia and Georgia Railway Company, under its equipment and improvement mortgage
of 1888 and its general mortgage of 1890. Those and
other properties embraced under the West Point Company were, under these foreclosures, bid in by the
Southern Railway Company, subject to underlying
liens. Exchange of bonds and shares of these foreclosed companies for those of the new company were
proceeded with according to the plan of reorganization,
the suits for foreclosure being carried out without opposition to transfer the title.

But since railways fill so large a part in our modern
industrial life and since we can safely say that there

must be carriers of traffic so long as civilization en-
dures, it is apparent that that traffic can be made the
security for the borrowing of money as safely and
legitimately as can a dwelling-house ; provided always
that those rules of financiering are observed which
require only that the minimum value of the property
be represented by such funded debts. The investor,
therefore, need not fear to put his money into railway
bonds or debentures because of the commercial conditions under which railways are operated ; but those
commercial conditions require that he should, if he
seek safety for his investment, consider the bearing of
these facts upon the particular road in which he is
interested. If the earning capacity of that company
becomes for any reason impaired, the strong legal language of the mortgage will not save the holder of the
company's bonds from loss. In the end he must accept
as a basis for revaluation of his securities the earning
power of the company as a carrier of traffic.

When money is loaned upon a dwelling-house the
mortgage is made to cover the real estate as security,
the bond which usually accompanies the mortgage
being a contract under which the mortgagor pledges
all his property for the repayment of the loan. The
terms have a slightly different meaning, however,
when applied to corporations. The mortgage is the
indenture issued by the company to trustees who may
be trust companies or individuals. The preference for
trust companies as trustees under these mortgages
arises from the fact that their existence is continuous,
that they have all the machinery for properly execut-
ing large transactions, and because their names are
known to all investors.

The mortgage made to trustees contains the terms

under which the money is borrowed. Under this mortgage and governed by its terms the Company issues bonds of the denomination stated in the instrument, usually $1000, which bonds may be registered with the interest payable by check, or may be coupon bonds accompanied with sheets of coupons that when cut off on the respective interest dates are payable to bearer as drafts upon the company and so easily collectible. The one form of bond or the other is preferred according as the holder wishes to make a permanent investment secured against theft or destruction, though the sale of a registered bond is a matter requiring some little time and trouble—or prefers a form which, in the language of Wall Street, is a " good delivery " for instant sale at any time.

The railway mortgage usually begins by giving the name of the company with the particulars of its incorporation ; then follows an exhaustive list of the property to be mortgaged. If there are prior liens upon the property or on any part of it, these exceptions are stated. Then the amount for which the mortgage is to be issued is stated, and the purposes for which the money is to be used should be given in detail. Then may be stated the procedure under which the trustee is allowed to certify bonds for sale to the public. The object of appointing a trustee is to see that the legal formalities embodied in the mortgage are strictly carried out, and that there is no over-issue. The mortgage often contains a provision exempting the trustee from all liability under any circumstances. Sometimes the bonds are to be certified by the trustee from time to time merely on the resolution of the Board of Directors ; but the more modern mortgages deny this power of issue until certain forms are observed. For instance,

in the case of bonds on a road under construction it is
often provided that no new bond shall be issued until
a certificate is filed with the trustee, signed by the
president and chief engineer, certifying that the
stated number of miles of road have been completed
and turned over to the operating department.

In cases where there are existing underlying liens it
is sometimes provided in the mortgage that these
underlying bonds shall be paid off as they mature and
not extended ; this is done in order to insure to the
issuing bonds a first lien at the maturity of the underlying mortgages. In late mortgages, some sections
relating to reorganization in case of insolvency have
been inserted. The sections referring to the foreclosure
of the mortgage are usually very carefully considered.
A common arrangement is that in case of non-payment
of interest, when such a default continues for six
months, at the request of a certain small proportion of
the bondholders, the trustee may begin foreclosure proceedings or enter upon the possession of the property ;
or in case of a demand by a considerable percentage of
the bondholders, shall do so. In that way practical
control of the foreclosure proceedings is given to a certain proportion of the holders of the bonds outstanding.
A few of the older mortgages give this power of controlling foreclosures to a small proportion (the old general
mortgage of the Philadelphia and Reading granted the
privilege to ten per cent. of the outstanding bonds),
but the later mortgages require a larger percentage.
Another interesting feature in modern mortgages,
inserted because of certain experience in that direction,
allows the trustees under certain circumstances to withdraw the proceedings for foreclosure, if such have been
begun, where a more favorable outcome would be had

by compromise, or where a technical default should not allow the company to pay off an established and secure mortgage not yet due, for the sake of refunding the loan, in that compulsory fashion, at a lower rate of interest. It is also well to give to the majority of the bonds outstanding—say three fourths—the power to direct a trustee to buy in the property at foreclosure in accordance with any plan or reorganization which may be adopted, and also under certain circumstances to authorize the creation of new mortgages prior to the one under consideration. These latter features are in the mortgage of the Southern Railway Company.

Since the provisions of the mortgage govern the whole transaction, and since a mistake here may have disastrous consequences, it is the usual custom to employ good corporation lawyers, so that the terms of the mortgage may be formulated in strict accordance with the equities of the case. On the one side the stockholders, as well as the company itself, desire that the conditions of the mortgage shall be as little onerous as possible; on the other hand, the lenders wish the mortgage drawn so as to give them the best security. Just where the line of compromise shall fall depends to a certain extent upon the reputation of the company and its general credit. On the other hand, where provisions of the mortgage are too loosely drawn, they may defeat their own purpose in not allowing money to be borrowed by the corporation at the most favorable rates and under the most favorable conditions.

Mortgages are divided into classes and called by various names according as their claim upon the property is direct or indirect. Prior lien bonds need no particular discussion. Our present railway systems have been formed in most cases out of a number of existing roads. In a great many instances these older and smaller companies have issued bonds which are necessarily the first mortgage upon their respective portions. These senior bonds, as they are sometimes called, may be liens upon old roads which are now parts of the new main line and worth many times the original mortgage. Such underlying bonds, having been issued years ago, often bear six per cent. or seven per cent. interest, and being considered thoroughly secure, sell on the exchanges at such prices as yield the investor but a small return. Upon the system as a whole there may be a first mortgage, so called because it is the first mortgage of the consolidated company, although the prior lien bonds just mentioned of course take precedence of it. After the first mortgage other bonds may come. A form of bond which was at one time popular but afterwards fell into partial disrepute, is the income or preference bond. The bond is so called because it attempts to combine the lien of a mortgage with contingency of interest. The mortgage in due form declares the principal to be a claim upon the property, but follows this statement with another, that no interest shall be paid unless it has been earned. In most cases the question whether there shall be any net earnings applicable to this interest in any given year is left absolutely to the discretion of the Board of Directors. A fatal objection to the income or preference bond is that it is an attempt to combine two contradictory commercial principles. As we have already seen, the lender of money to a corporation does not wish to participate either in the profits or the losses arising from the success or failure of the company, but simply intends to loan his money on what he thinks is sufficient security, so that he may receive the interest on the same and the principal when due. To the stockholders who manage the company are left the profits or losses over and above this charge upon the minimum value of the property, whichever these may be. It will be noticed that security for both interest and principal is the essence of the creditor's position, while contingency depending upon success is the essence of the stockholder's position. We might, therefore, expect that a so-called bond which attempts to combine security with contingency would prove disappointing to all concerned, and so it has turned out. In some cases income bonds have been given to old security holders in part payment for sacrifices which they were asked to make because of former insolvency. In such cases it would have been better had these old holders accepted their changed position from creditors to partners and received preferred stock for their deferred claims. The income bonds of the Atchison, Topeka and Santa Fé, issued after the reorganization of 1889, and the preference bonds of the Philadelphia and Reading, issued after the reorganization of 1886, are instances of such bonds. A practical objection often raised to income bonds by British and German holders of such bonds, is that the Board of Directors representing the shareholders may in years of good earnings put into the property the surplus revenues which might have gone toward paying interest on the income bonds, and continue such a policy until such time as the earnings of the company justify paying interest to the income holders and at the same time a dividend on stock. Against such appropriation of the earnings, when equitably due to them, the income holders have usually no remedy. Sometimes the power of voting has been given to such bonds in order to guard against such a possible abuse ; but preferred stock is a better thing to issue and to hold under these circumstances than the miscalled income bond.

In our corporation history there have been instances of preference bonds, like those of the Philadelphia and Reading, with the definition of net earnings applicable to their payment drawn in the mortgage of 1888 in such severe terms that there seemed no loophole of escape. Nevertheless charges have in such cases been ingeniously put ahead of such bonds. It may happen, too, that the very severity of the language which is intended to compel the payment to the preferred holder. of all earnings over and above certain specified and fixed charges, by defeating other borrowings or by depriving the company of improvement moneys, may so embarrass the managers of the company as to cause the preference bonds themselves to fall in value.

Another form of corporation borrowing of which we have seen instances in late years, is that of collateral bonds or trust notes. Collateral bonds are obligations issued by a company with a lien upon the real estate junior to that of other mortgages. To give these collateral bonds value in the eyes of investors they are made a first lien upon various bonds and stocks, usually of auxiliary companies, which are taken from the treasury of the system and deposited with some trust company as trustee under the terms of the collateral mortgage. As the name implies, such a mortgage is really a borrowing upon the collateral owned by the company, and differs from the borrowing of money from the banks through the hypothecation of the securities in the company's treasury, only by arranging for a loan for a term of years and at a fixed rate under certain specified conditions.

A large system which has been formed by the consolidation from time to time with it of various other and smaller corporations usually finds that it has collected in its treasury a considerable number of bonds or shares which represent to it its investments for control. These bonds or shares are those of railroad companies whose corporate existence may still be kept up, but which form nevertheless an integral part of the present system ; or they may be the bonds or shares of terminal companies, or warehouse or elevator companies, or of some water transportation company which provides by river or lake an important connection with the present company ; or, of companies which furnish much traffic to the railroads, and whose securities were bought in order that that traffic may be held for the system beyond a doubt. In all these cases it is assumed that the continuance of the control of the parent company over the various enterprises whose bonds and shares it holds is necessary to the preservation of the system and to the securing to the system of the traffic represented. To pledge these various shares and bonds for a new loan is regarded as legitimate financiering because it grants to the holders of the collateral bonds a claim upon the assets of the company, a claim which often in effect, though not in name, is equal to that of regular mortgage bonds.

An illustration of such mortgages by a strong company is that of the four per cent. extension bonds of the Chicago and Northwestern Railway Company, issued in 1886, upon the bonds of the branch road, the Fremont, Elkhorn, and Missouri Valley, deposited with the trustee as collateral. In like manner the Illinois Central Railroad Company in 1888 issued collateral bonds based upon the deposit with the trustee of various bonds of subsidiary roads important to the system. The uncertainty of the value of a claim upon collateral in cases of insolvency is illustrated by the history of the collateral trust bonds of the Oregon Short Line and Utah Northern Company. This company, under the control of the Union Pacific, purchased more than half the stock of the Oregon Railway and Navigation Company (a connecting road), and, depositing the same with the trustee, issued thereon its collateral trust bonds. Pending the reorganization of the Union Pacific and because of a decline in the earnings of the Oregon Railway and Navigation Company, the value of these collateral trust bonds became but nominal. In 1883 the Wabash, St. Louis, and Pacific issued $6,000,000 of collateral trust bonds bearing six per cent. interest and sold them to the public at 90. Under the reorganization of this company into the Wabash Railroad Company (dating from July, 1889) these collateral trust bonds were exchanged into debenture " B " bonds of the new company, the latter being quoted at less than one third of the price at which the collateral trust bonds were originally issued and sold.

The difficulty which experience has found with collateral bonds lies in the fluctuating value of the securities pledged under them. The collateral bond held by the public is a mortgage upon certain other mortgages, and if foreclosed by reason of insolvency the purchasers legally come into possession, not of the real estate of the company, but of certain other bonds, which in turn may have to be foreclosed separately, necessitating a large number of distinct actions. The loss is the same whether these separate transactions are actually carried out or an equivalent reduction made in the quoted values of the bonds. Not only is the expense of the transaction and the ultimate outcome made doubtful by these facts, but in securing the absolute property delays which may occur under these circumstances may cause further losses ; for it is plain that the value of the subsidiary properties whose bonds and shares are pledged as collateral may depend, in cases where the mortgaging company becomes bankrupt, largely upon the quickness with which they may be seized upon and handled with vigor by their new owners. In a developing country new discoveries in mining may be made, or new centres for trade distribution or manufacturing may be formed, which may change the value to the system of a branch line or auxiliary company so materially and so rapidly, that holders of a funded obligation resting for security upon these subsidiary properties may find their real security slipping away from them while they are yet helpless. For these reasons a collateral bond usually ranks in quotations below that of other mortgages of the same company covering specific portions of its property.

But while these remarks are true in many cases there are instances, like those of the Chicago and Northwestern and Illinois Central, to which they do not practically apply. There are railways which have been in operation for many years and whose traffic not only as to volume but as to source has become well established. Fluctuations in the value of the properties directly owned by such companies are so little likely to occur that collateral bonds issued upon the stocks and bonds of such subsidiary properties are a comparatively safe investment. There is no hard and fast rule for judging of the lien in these cases. Each company and each collateral mortgage must be valued by the merits in each particular case. The general reputation and credit of the mortgaging company should also be taken into consideration.

The objections raised to collateral bonds before spoken of have led to variations in the form intended to meet these difficulties. Such a variation is that of collateral trust notes. Like collateral bonds these notes are an obligation of the issuing company and are made a first lien upon certain shares and bonds of properties important to the system, which are given to some trust company to be held as collateral for the notes. With this difference, however, that the mortgage gives the control of the hypothecated bonds and shares to a particular trust company or to a committee of financiers, who have the power to dispose of these hypothecated bonds and shares under circumstances which are carefully stated in the mortgage. Sometimes authority is given to this committee to sell these hypothecated securities at certain stipulated prices or at their discretion, the proceeds of the sale being used to redeem the collateral notes ; or else the committee are empowered to make such sales either of all or of part of the securities as they may deem best, in case of a forfeiture of interest payments by the obligating company. These provisions, with others of the same tenor, are inserted in the collateral trust mortgage in order to do away with the objections of investors and by making the transaction more nearly like the ordinary borrowings of money at the banks, to command a higher price for these notes than would otherwise be obtainable. Examples may be found in the issues of collateral trust notes by the Union Pacific and Northern Pacific Companies in 1891 and 1893.

Railway systems which have attained their present magnitude either through the consolidation of parts of

their road at different times or through the amalgamation at one time of a number of smaller companies,
often find themselves obliged to provide new capital in
order to arrange for improvements necessary for handling a larger amount of business, improvements which
are required in order to introduce the very economies in
operating for which the combination may have been
formed. In a developing country like the United
States the demand for railway capital, except in periods
of depression, is continuous. As traffic grows so must
facilities increase. And since it has heretofore been
our experience that an increase in the number of passengers and tons of freight is accompanied by a decrease in the amount received per passenger or per ton,
an American road should be considered well managed
if the net earnings, legitimately arrived at, increase a
little faster than the fixed charges. Such a result, if
fairly obtained, proves that the additional capital spent
upon the property from year to year has been product-
ive. Acknowledging that systems require the expenditure of money, it often becomes a problem upon what
special security this money should be raised. One
method is that of issuing " blanket " mortgages, as
they are called, a Wall Street term which means merely
that the system which already has prior mortgages
upon different parts of it, now issues bonds which cover
the system as a whole, subject, of course, to the underlying encumbrances upon the property.

In the minds of financial men some of these blanket
mortgages do not hold a first-class position ; the feeling
against them may be summed up thus : blanket bonds
are not first mortgages—a fact which everyone must
admit. Yet if it is true that systems must grow, just
as parts of the same system increased while inde-

4

pendent, there is much to be said in justification of
obtaining capital by bonding the system as a whole.
The majority of the things needed by the system are
such as are chargeable upon the separate parts only
proportionately. Equipment which is bought for the
benefit of the system should not be paid for by the further issue of divisional bonds, even where such additional issues are provided for in the divisional mortgage.
So, too, bonds sold for the acquisition of freight yards
are intended to facilitate the handling of traffic over the
whole system. In the approaching days when the use
of air-brakes for freight trains and of one pattern of
freight-car coupler will increase the number of trains
which may be moved rapidly and safely over any particular piece of road, the capacity of the terminals rather
than that of the track will even more than at present
prove the standard by which the limit to the volume
of traffic will be measured. It would be unjust under
these present or supposed future circumstances to
charge the cost of such terminals to that part of the
whole system upon which they may happen to be
located. There is no way of meeting these demands
so equitably as by the issue of system bonds for system
improvements. Blanket mortgages have been issued by
the Chicago, Milwaukee, and St. Paul and the Louisville, and Nashville Railway Companies, among others.

If these blanket mortgages are carefully drawn with
provisions compelling the retirement of the prior liens
as such mature, they will in time become first mortgages themselves. Some modern blanket mortgages
also contain sections limiting the amount of bonds
which may be issued for improvement in any one year,
the intention being to prevent the forcing upon the
market of such an issue of bonds as to cause a decline

in price, and also to check a yearly issue in excess of reasonable requirements. An example of such a guarded mortgage covering an issue of blanket or system bonds is that of the Cleveland, Cincinnati, Chicago, and St. Louis general mortgage of 1893.

If corporations become insolvent it is expected that such blanket or general bonds will be the first to be seriously affected. The Wabash, St. Louis, and Pacific Company in 1880 issued and sold $16,000,000 of its six per cent. " general " or system bonds at 95. Becoming bankrupt, a new corporation, the Wabash Railroad Company, was formed in 1889. The general bonds of the old company were converted into debenture " B " bonds of the new company, these being quoted at less than one third of the price at which the generals were originally sold.

There is no doubt that blanket mortgages may lend themselves to over-colored notions of future possible traffic sometimes held by optimistic managers. The ease with which such bonds may be issued to the large amounts for which the mortgages are made sometimes proves too tempting to railway officers who, through good motives or bad, venture upon extravagant calculations of the growth in business for the future. In such cases blanket bonds are not regarded much more highly than would be the same amount of preferred stock. While this, however, is a danger, it is not a good argument against system bonds when legitimately issued. Blanket bonds should be judged, therefore, by that principle in general debt financiering which requires the amount of borrowed money to be well within the minimum value of the property. When this requirement is kept in view, and when the company has been operating its lines of railway long enough to allow a fair estimate as to the stability of the traffic, the issue of blanket or system bonds is proper and safe.

One form of railway mortgages differing somewhat from those which have just been considered, is that of terminal bonds. Mortgages upon terminal properties which are indispensable to the successful operation of railways are generally well regarded by investors. Proper terminals are more and more essential to our railways as the commercial development of the country proceeds. Passenger stations in important cities, with the land necessary for approaching tracks, are necessary if a company is to continue in business and not to yield its traffic to some rival ; and mortgages upon such properties are well thought of. Mortgages upon some railway terminals at Chicago and New York are examples. There are other terminal bonds, however, which cover cases not precisely similar to the one just mentioned. Terminal properties which are used or may be used by two, three, or more railroads sometimes depend for their immediate value upon the question whether their facilities are, or in the near future can be, fully utilized ; or whether one or more of the occupying companies may not transfer their favors to some other terminal property more accessible to their lines. These inquiries embrace also another set of facts ; whether the properties covered by the mortgage under consideration are the best that can be had and whether they are therefore from that point of view also sure of continued occupancy. The case of the Chicago and Northern Pacific Company is an illustration. This company acquired lands, tracks, and other terminal properties in the city of Chicago, and in 1890 authorized an issue of $30,000,000 five per cent. bonds. It was admitted that the properties covered by the mortgage were of great

value of themselves, but because of lack of tenants fully
to utilize their facilities, on the appointment of receivers
for the Northern Pacific and Wisconsin Central Companies in 1893 (companies which had practically guaranteed bond interest), the Chicago and Northern Pacific
was likewise placed in the hands of receivers, its bonds
falling in price to one half their former quotations.

In other cases railway companies have themselves
issued terminal bonds which they make a first lien on
certain specific terminal properties of their own. In
such instances the value of the grounds and buildings
in cities must be judged according to the hints already
given. If such bonds, however, cover terminals in
towns or villages remote from cities or away from
places which from the traffic point of view may be
called strategic, the question may arise whether the
land thus set apart for country terminals has any
special value for railroad purposes. If the company
could easily put down elsewhere tracks and buildings
suitable for their purpose, then their so-called terminal
bonds are dependent for their value not so much on the
property mortgaged as upon the general success of the
company as a carrier of traffic.

Some of the older of our railway mortgages provide
for a sinking fund. The sections relating to such funds
usually provide that a certain sum shall be set apart
annually and paid to the mortgage trustees. These
sums are to be invested in the company's bonds of the
issue to be thus retired, either by purchase in the open
market or more commonly at a price fixed in the mortgage, the particular bonds required being drawn by lot
and the result advertised in the daily papers. The
bonds thus chosen cease drawing public interest. It is
usually also provided in such cases that the bonds pur-

chased by lot shall not be cancelled but remain alive
(that is, remain in all their original force against the
company) in the hands of the mortgage trustee, the
interest on them being added to the sinking fund and
used in the purchase of further outstanding bonds.
By this method it is not difficult to calculate the exact
annual payments by the company which will be necessary in order that the mortgage trustee at the maturity
of the mortgage may have on hand the amount of
money required to pay all interest and principal and
thus cancel the whole issue.

It is sometimes provided that the money contributed
by the company to form a sinking fund may be used to
purchase other bonds of the same system in case the
bonds in question cannot be had at a named price ; or
perhaps the whole matter is left to the discretion of the
trustee or of the company's directors.   It usually happens that the quotations of such sinking-fund bonds are
higher than the purchase price named in the sinking-
fund sections of the mortgage, and hence the investment of the fund in other securities is necessary.

The course followed in such cases is to buy such
other bonds, perhaps of subsidiary roads, as will indeed
make up the par value required at maturity, but whose
value depends upon the fact that they are obligations
of the selfsame system.   Such bonds—or indeed any
bonds other than the issues originally intended to be
extinguished by the sinking fund—could not be sold to
the public without increasing the interest charges payable to the public by the amount of the interest on the
old bonds.   In this way the owners of the old bonds
indeed receive their principal and interest, but the fixed
charges of the system are not in any wise reduced by
the transaction.   Sometimes it is thought desirable for

the company to take over into the treasury all these securities held in the funds, the maturing issues being meanwhile met by sales of other bonds of the same company which bear a lower rate of interest or are part of a larger mortgage and already sure of a market. In such cases the labor of keeping up the sinking fund is thrown away, because usually the exchange of the new bond for the old could have been easily accomplished without that machinery.

When railway companies are in good credit, or when the mortgage containing sinking-fund clauses covers property conceded to be worth more than the bonds, the establishment of such funds is a financial mistake. If the bonds are to be compulsorily retired so many each year by lot at say 110 per cent. of their par value, that fact immediately decreases their value as investments. No investor likes to buy bonds which, however good or whatever the premium he may have paid for them, he may have to give up a short time after purchasing. If a bond is really good, the longer the time it has to run the better the bond-buyers like it. Another practical objection is that no one wishes to be on the lookout for advertisements which he may or may not chance to see, but which are legal notices binding on the bondholder that interest on the bonds named by their numbers ceases on a certain date.

On the other hand, the companies would rightly object to a sinking-fund system which should require them to contribute certain sums yearly to be used in buying that particular issue of bonds in the open market. Such a provision would soon create an artificial scarcity in those bonds so that the price quotations would be above the normal. To purchase at a high premium bonds which at maturity the company could pay at par would be poor financiering, and a use of the current revenues of the company to which the shareholders could properly object. The form of sinking fund which allows of the investment of the funds in securities other than those intended to be retired, is of little practical value to the bondholders in question. Their mortgage is upon a certain piece of property, and that is still their main hope. It usually happens that the securities purchased by such a fund are those of the same system, and thus at maturity it is often found that to pay off one obligation there is nothing in the fund but another obligation of the same company ; and if the first is not itself good, the other is not likely to be worth much. Investments of sinking funds in bonds of other enterprises are not favored for obvious reasons, while purchases of such undoubted securities as government bonds at high premiums would cost the company and the bond- and shareholders more than the accruing benefits. For these reasons, sinking-fund requirements have been left out of most of our modern railway mortgages. As to companies in poor credit, whose bonds rule very low in price, there is not much to be said. Corporation financiering requires that debts shall be only of such a proportion to the real value as will bring the highest returns to the company with the lowest rate of interest. Sinking funds do not need discussion where different conditions prevail. As such funds can be accumulated from but one source—the revenues of the company, and as under our present supposition, those reserves are not enough to sustain the bond credit, it is practically useless to rely upon them for the formation of any such thing as a sinking fund. Companies in distress will always use current revenues to

pay pressing needs regardless of sinking-fund clauses
in their mortgages.

Since under practical conditions sinking funds in
the mortgages of railways having good credit are not
favored, we may next inquire as to the public aspect of
the matter. In national finance it is now understood
that sinking funds for the payment of government
bonds can be established only from governmental revenues ; in short, from taxes. If, therefore, it be the
opinion that the government should not remain always
in debt, but arrange to pay off its borrowings by degrees, the funds must be supplied from taxes. The
government is not in business and has no business revenues. But corporations which, so far as we now see,
must continue to earn money through their services to
the public indefinitely, occupy a different place. The
rules covering public debt financiering do not now
apply. Rather do we see the opposite, where borrowing is not only a necessity, but often the only road to
success. The revenues of such corporations do not
come from taxes, but from moneys given to them in
return for services rendered in a business way to those
concerned. Such services must in some form be continuous, and the benefits paid for continuously on a
business basis. Moreover, through competition or in
other ways, the profits of such companies tend toward
smaller margins, these being usually only enough to
pay a fair return to the capital invested. Since the
only way to pay off debts is from revenue, it follows
that the retirement of bonds at maturity by cash payment (except, of course, through the sale of other
bonds) could be effected only by increasing the revenues
through advancement of the prices charged to passengers and shippers, or by the shareholders (or perhaps

the bondholders themselves) foregoing their returns for years. As a practical matter either way is unadvisable or impossible. Unlike taxes, rates or prices could not be advanced so largely as to pay off bonded debts. Railway charges, for example, could not be increased to that extent in the face of an adverse public opinion. On the other hand, to stop dividends for such a purchase would prove equally unpopular, and would also result in a decay of public progress in our industries ; for no one would undertake a new enterprise if he were not permitted to reap the annual fruits of his ability and labor.

For these reasons the payment of corporation debts from corporation revenues is, generally speaking, impossible in practice. Hence it is assumed—by large railway systems, for illustration—that when an existing mortgage matures the company will be able to borrow new money to pay off the old, and perhaps at a lower rate of interest. Sinking funds for such a purpose are unnecessary, though, as a matter of formal obligation, they may be kept up by companies in good credit, like the Chicago, Burlington, and Quincy or Chicago and Northwestern. But reference has been made to corporations which it is assumed will go on doing a stable business indefinitely. Other companies may be subject to extreme fluctuations in profits, or, like mining corporations, may have a certain number of years to run when their business opportunities will be exhausted. In such cases sinking funds fulfil a proper purpose— that of guarding the interests of the mortgagees, and should be insisted upon ; such funds may be established either by way of deposit with trustees of moneys to purchase bonds or be held in trust, or by writing off the values of the plant before paying dividends and holding such moneys in a sort of depreciation account, or by a combination of both methods. There is no real confusion between indefinite and short-lived companies, for by a commercial law the short-lived corporation may retain a rate of profit on its transactions high enough, if well managed, for all sinking-fund purposes, and higher than anything which the stable corporation may hope to gain. A business which bears no evidence of stability and endurance, or whose life, if it is to be short, cannot be calculated and provided for, should not become incorporated. The partnership form is best adapted to enterprises which are largely speculative in character.

In order to draw capital from all sources, corporation mortgages are made to trustees who certify to certain bonds of small denominations. In this way the borrowings of corporations, amounting in some cases to more than a hundred million dollars at a time, are divided into small sums within the reach of the humble investor. Of late years the trust companies in the Eastern cities have been selected as trustees instead of individuals whenever the law of the State where the property was situated allowed of such selection. Trust companies have manifold advantages over individuals in such a relationship; they do not die; the large amount of financial business which they daily transact provides them with the machinery for such purposes; while their well-known names stand as evidence to the purchasing public that at least the necessary formalities have been complied with. Beyond that responsibility the trustees of corporation mortgages usually assume none.

In recent years the trust companies have shown a tendency, when acting as mortgage trustees, to recognize a greater moral responsibility than they at first were willing to bear. Trust companies did not, of course, intend to appear as in any way guaranteeing the bonds to which they certified, though that seems often to have been the erroneous opinion of the unthinking ; but trustees now acknowledge themselves bound within the limits of the mortgage to use their influence to protect the interests of the bondholders. A trust company which should now allow the issue of unsecured bonds because of some glaring defect in the language of the mortgage, would no longer be morally excused by financial opinion, though perhaps held technically innocent.

One way in which this sentiment attributing some sort of ethical responsibility to trustees of corporation mortgages manifests itself is through slight alterations in the wording of the mortgage itself. The old language was that the trustee was to be held harmless under all circumstances. Now the trustee is often found willing to assume responsibility at least for gross negligence or for the negligence of servants or clerks not carefully selected. If to some such phrases be added a more careful drawing of the mortgage as to its provisions against unauthorized issues of bonds, a better compliance with the ethics of the situation would be had ; for it is undeniable that a part of the public complaint against the fraudulent issue of bonds should be directed against the inadequate safeguards imposed in the mortgage rather than against the trustee.

As an example of what is meant may be taken a mortgage which we will say may be issued for the purpose of improving a railroad, though the proceeds of the bond when sold may be devoted toward an entirely different object, one, we will say, tainted with

fraud. Such a fraudulent misuse of company borrowings would be checked at the outset if the mortgage
had contained sections limiting the amount of money
which should be expended in any one year, and providing that the trustees should not certify to any of
the bonds until a certificate had been filed with the
trust company, signed by the chief engineer, stating
that a certain amount of work had been done or a
certain number of miles of new road or new track con-
structed. This statement of the chief engineer could
have been accompanied by an affidavit, signed by the
president and treasurer of the company, to the effect
that the allegations of the chief engineer were true.
Provisions of this character, varied according to the
circumstances of each case, but to the same intent,
should be inserted in every mortgage which contem-
plates the spending of new money for corporation uses.
Restrictions such as these would protect the trustee ;
while at the same time rendering the officers clearly
responsible to the public and to the law for any lapse
of corporation duty as to any issue of bonds whenever
a fraudulent or unauthorized use of the money was
thus guarded against. The two ideas of better care on
the part of the trustees of corporation mortgages, and
of better definition of the terms and conditions under
which the money is to be borrowed and used, go together. Both are essential unless we are willing to
entrust the whole matter to the good faith and to the
interpretation put upon responsibility by those concerned. The necessity of granting to the directors
chosen by the stockholders to manage the property, at
least a proper amount of liberty in that management
is obvious ; but that concerns the shareholders, not the
creditors. Good corporation financiering requires that

money be borrowed on the best possible terms. Since bondholders do not wish to concern themselves with questions of success or failure in management, they are best pleased with investments which are surrounded with all possible money safeguards. Cheap borrowing demands that the prejudices of capitalists be, within all reasonable limits, regarded.

The listing of bonds and shares on the exchanges is of benefit to both corporations and investors. A wider market is thus made for those who wish to buy or to sell. One of the advantages of corporation securities, and one which gives to them a higher range of values than they otherwise would obtain, is the ease and rapidity with which sales can be made. Real estate, for instance, with all its good points, has the drawback that it cannot be quickly turned into cash at need. In like manner a mortgage on country property cannot be used at the banks as collateral for loans, nor can a mortgage on good city property always be easily disposed of. Bonds and shares of corporations which can be listed on the exchanges have at once a standing (not value) which gives them a market at some price always. Corporations which issue bonds and shares intended for public purchase, should list such issues whenever possible.

CHAPTER IV.

SUBSIDIARY COMPANIES AND THEIR SECURITIES.

OUR American systems of railways are matters of growth. They usually consist of a number of smaller roads once independent which have been joined together by purchase or by consolidation. Where these lines are continuous their status does not need discussion. The original bonds of such lines are recognized as having a prior lien which cannot be disputed, and as such they command very high quotations on the stock exchanges; but in addition to old roads which now form a part of the existing main line, nearly all our systems have branch roads, which at greater or less length reach from the main line into some agricultural section or to mines or to cities. In this way facilities of transportation are afforded to the sections thus reached, while the main-line traffic is increased. It is only lately that the importance of well-located branch lines to the main stem has been appreciated in the public mind. The capacity of the main line of a railway for carrying a large quantity of traffic is very great, being practically limited only by the amplitude of the terminals. Every additional car which may be added to trains that must be run in any case is a clear gain to the company; in like manner the receipts from every additional freight train which the road may receive up to the limit of its capacity are also direct gains after deducting the train or " movement " expenses ; for while the latter may be roughly estimated at forty cents a train mile, the average gross earnings of such a train in the United States are about $1.60 per mile run. The increasing profitableness and necessity of additional traffic explains why the railways in the United States, and particularly those doing a small business west of the Mississippi River, have been led either to build branch roads into all sections where extra traffic might profitably be secured or to support directly or indirectly so many auxiliary businesses, farming or stock-raising enterprises, which might add to the volume of traffic. So clear has the necessity of branch lines seemed to the managers of the railways in our newer States that the company which did not build or purchase subsidiary enterprises might not expect to develop traffic in the parts of the country near their lines ; indeed, could not hope to hold their shipments against the competing railways which were active in following out the policy of building such lines.

The profit accruing to the main lines from the traffic which they interchanged with the branch railroads was great in any case, and became all the more conspicuously so when, as usually happened, the main line was benefited by the long haul of hundreds of miles upon this branch-line business. Sometimes these branch railroads proved very expensive to build, as, for example, in attempts to reach some mountain mining camp ; and whether expensive or not, the money for their construction was usually obtained by the issue of branch-line bonds, which may have been guaranteed directly by the parent company or were made salable to the public by a lease or other contract, setting forth in some form the obligation of the large road to its dependency. The majority of the branch roads in the old Northern Pacific system, for illustration, were operated under leases which specified that the earnings of the branch, even though prorated mile for mile, should always be equal to the annual sums required for bond interest and sinking funds. .

Where such branch lines were built with reasonable judgment and care there seems no doubt that their building was justified. Under the circumstances a division of the joint earnings on the basis of mile for mile of the whole distance carried would be, as a criterion of its real value, manifestly unfair to the subsidiary road. It has been determined by railroad custom for many years that the division of joint earnings between two companies should be on equal terms only when the circumstances were equal. But when the little road is the originator of the traffic, receiving that traffic from different stations in small lots and delivering it at the junction point in train loads to the main line, it is well settled that the conditions are not equal, and that the branch line is commercially entitled to more than its mileage proportion of the through rate. With a few of its branches just mentioned, the Northern Pacific arranged to allow a concession of two miles on the branch for every mile actually travelled. In some cases of short branch lines these have been allowed to charge arbitraries, as they are called, *i. e.*, fixed sums regardless of the through rate, sums fixed high enough to yield the auxiliary road fair earnings. In other cases these branches have been allowed " constructive " mileage, through either an agreed percentage of the whole rate, or a proportion based upon two or three times the actual length of the haul upon the branch line. As an illustration of the division of earn-

5

ings by fixed percentages, the case of the lines of the
Atchison, Topeka, and Santa Fé system in California
may be taken. At the time of the Atchison receivership in December, 1893, on shipments of freight from
Los Angeles, California, to Kansas City, Missouri, five
cents per hundred pounds were allowed as a terminal
charge in Los Angeles; the California lines were
(after deducting the terminal charge) then credited
with nineteen per cent. of the through revenue. The
remainder of the through charge was then divided on a
mileage basis between the other roads in the system
carrying the traffic. On a mile-for-mile basis the California lines would have received but about eight per
cent. of the total charge. An example of purely constructive mileage is that of the allowance by the Union
Pacific main line to the Oregon Short Line (a part of
the Union Pacific system) of 1¾ miles for each one
mile of actual haul. To show the results of constructive mileage in practice a supposititious case may be
taken. If a branch road is one hundred miles long and
the freight which it originates is hauled a distance of
five hundred miles on the main line (the freight
charges being based in the first place upon the commercial conditions), strict mileage proportion would
require that the branch road should receive one sixth
of the total charges. If the constructive mileage of two
miles for one were allowed to the auxiliary roads its
haul would be considered as two hundred miles for the
purpose of the calculations, the main line having the
same mileage as before, five hundred miles; this would
give the little road two sevenths of the same total
receipts. Out of joint earnings, amounting to $1000,
the former method would give the branch $166.67,
while constructive mileage of two for one would yield

$285.71, the difference, $119.04, being a net increase—that is, an increase of earnings without an increase of expenses. Sometimes three miles for one are allowed the auxiliary company. But few branches have so long a proportionate haul as one hundred miles. In cases where the distance to the junction of the main line is very short, the branch is allowed in the calculations a minimum distance of say fifty miles. It occasionally happens that roads having a long mileage are by reason of their circumstances really to be considered in the light of branches and entitled to more than a strict mileage proportion of the revenues received from the traffic carried over their own and other lines on a through rate. The case of the Oregon Short Line, just cited, is an example. What proportions are equitable in any particular case can only be determined by a careful study of all the circumstances, and by consulting the judgment of those who by long experience are familiar with the customs of the railways in these respects.

When the Chicago, Burlington, and Quincy Railroad was built west of the Mississippi River, the Nebraska lines received half of the through rate for the average haul of 135 miles, as against the other half received by the old main line for its haul of 486 miles. Illustrations of this sort abound in our railroad history. Nor are they new. A dozen years ago the legislature of Illinois investigated the practice of the Illinois Central Railroad in allowing constructive mileage to its branches, on complaint that the State, which was entitled to seven per cent. of the gross earnings of that company, was by this policy losing the sums due to it. The committee reported that this method of encouraging the building of branches by the Illinois Central really increased the revenues of the main line and therefore of the State. The case is even stronger than this. It was estimated by the United States Pacific Railway Commission in 1887 that, on the traffic interchanged by the Union Pacific Railway with its branches, the profit to the main line was in the aggregate nearly twice as much as that derived from the business originating on its own main lines. The testimony before that Commission was to the effect that without its system of branches the Union Pacific would have been then bankrupt.

Since the large systems were under the necessity of building or acquiring branch lines in order that their main lines might have a volume of traffic sufficient to make its carriage a financial success, it was soon seen that the position of these branches as regards the main stems must be defined commercially before the money for their building could be obtained. The owner of a branch-line bond was quick to see that he was dependent for the value of his property upon the main line ; for while the branch company held a contract of some sort with the parent company, the obligation of that contract came after the mortgages which had been or might be put upon the main lines, and hence might be disavowed in time of financial distress. Such a breach of contract would leave the branch-line holder without an adequate commercial remedy. In this way the necessity of putting a constructive valuation upon auxiliary properties, joined with the acknowledged business equities of the subject, led to the granting of a more or less defined position to subsidiary companies which could be sustained before the courts. Thus the holder of the bonds or other obligations of auxiliary companies was assured of a financial value to his holdings equivalent to their commercial value as ascertained by a consensus of railway opinion. This valuation being somewhat indefinite, the market quotations for the bonds of branch railway lines are influenced in part by the known advantages of the branch line in question, and in part by the general opinion as to the honor of the system managers and the ability of the company to earn the required revenues.

The necessity of branches, particularly in the developing sections of the country, being admitted, it follows that the values of those branches and the bonds upon them are not to be determined by the form of contract under which they are operated. In a large number of instances the exact commercial worth of each subsidiary company is not statistically worked out by the controlling system. It is often considered sufficient if a lease is made under which it is mutually agreed that the earnings of the branch shall always be equal to annual interest on the bonds. Then the joint earnings may be divided as may be most convenient for the bookkeeping, usually on a " straight mileage " basis, mile for mile. Under such accounting the branch line would show each year a deficit in earnings under fixed charges which under its lease the main company would take from its general treasury. Obviously such bookkeeping, though not intended to mislead, would not be a proper basis for estimating the commercial value of the branch property or of its bonds. At best it is a slovenly way of accounting. Usually it is adopted merely to save the trouble of obtaining expert opinion as to the true division of joint earnings. The books and statistics of large companies, railway or manufacturing, ought to be so kept and the public reports so made, as to show as exactly as possible the real earnings or losses of the system as a whole and of each particular branch line or subsidiary property not merged into the old company.

The inadequacy of this old style of accounting becomes of practical importance in cases of insolvency or where through the expiration of a lease a readjustment is to be made. The Board of Directors in the latter case may seek to compel the branch bondholders to accept a reduction in the interest rate to correspond with the earnings of the branch road as shown on the system's books. Or when a reorganization is necessary and the capitalization of the whole system must be reduced, the problem of dividing that reduction among all the obligations of the system becomes very complicated. If the real earnings of the different parts of the system are to be taken as the basis for the new capitalization, the holders of bonds of branch lines which show deficits may be asked to submit to many sacrifices of principal and interest. A case in point is that of the Atchison, Topeka, and Santa Fé system before referred to.   It will be remembered that the lines in California were allowed a fixed percentage—nineteen per cent.— of the through charge on shipments between Los Angeles, California, and Kansas City, Missouri, and that the remainder of the through charge was divided between the other carrying companies mile for mile. These other lines between the points named consisted of the Atlantic and Pacific from Barstow, California, to Albuquerque, New Mexico, about 747 miles, and the Atchison main line thence to Kansas City, about 920 miles. To secure the connecting line, the Atlantic and Pacific, the Atchison Company, jointly with another company, had guaranteed interest on the Atlantic bonds ; a necessary measure, for under the mile-for-mile contract and because of light local traffic and heavy operating expenses, this connecting line up to the date of the receivership had shown large deficits under fixed charges which were made good by the guarantors. When reorganization became necessary in 1895, the bondholders of the Atlantic and Pacific were unwilling to accept the deficits under the bookkeeping as proving the small value of their property, claiming that the commercial and fair worth had never been properly determined by the Atchison system when solvent. In such cases the only sure ground for determining the values of auxiliary properties or for refusing acquiescence in a new lease or in a reorganization plan, is the real commercial earning power or importance of the property in dispute. If such power has never been ascertained in the manner already indicated, the holders of bonds need not consent to a reduction until such appraisement has been made by competent authorities. There is every chance for fierce disputes at just this point ; for in cases of bankruptcy the owners of roads on the main lines naturally look upon their lien as paramount to obligations of any kind due to subsidiary companies ; and technically they are of course right. But the question at once arises : whence comes the traffic which, moving over the main lines, yields the earnings on which the senior mortgage has the first claim ? If from the stations on the main lines - if it is strictly " local "—the branch holders may be told to " take their road." But if, as often happens, the figures prove that an important part of this traffic is interchanged with branch roads, as in the case of the Union Pacific before mentioned, then those branch lines are entitled to an equitable share in the prosperity of the system whatever that may be ; a share to be decided by the proportion which branch-line earnings properly determined bear to the whole. For these reasons the real value of branch lines and branch-line bonds, when not settled until insolvency or termination of a lease, give rise to endless controversies. And yet the obligations of subsidiary companies when based upon values which by custom have come to have a substantial basis, are safe investments ; though those values ought to be established through accurate statistics from the very beginning.

It thus appears that branch lines are necessary to the development of the railway systems of our newer States and equally a necessity to the growth in wealth of the sections of the country traversed by them. It also appears that certain of these branches may have shown a yearly deficit under their own fixed charges, although the indirect benefits to the main lines may have been greater than the deficits paid from the company's treasury. In such case, however the accounts may be kept, the total result is a gain to the system. The question now arises, how should these deficits be treated in the company's books ? In some instances railways have preferred that the gross earnings should at first be reported as favorably to the main lines as possible in order that these might make a better showing. Sometimes controlling companies in making up their accounts for the year omitted those branch-line losses from their income statements, charging them instead as "loans" to subsidiary companies or as "investments" in branch-line bonds and stocks.

It would not be equitable to condemn every instance of this kind. If a reasonable expectation existed that the increase of traffic upon a new branch would in a year or two be such that the owning company would be reimbursed for such branch-line advances, the policy of carrying such deficits as loans for a short time might properly be followed. Instances may be found in the history of the Louisville and Nashville Railroad where some branch lines wisely projected but which did not yield in the first year or two direct income sufficient to pay the accruing bond interest, soon developed traffic enough to pay back to the parent company the full amount of all fixed charges from the beginning.

But railway managers are perforce optimistic, and share owners are naturally desirous of the best possible returns from their holdings ; so managers were led to continue the practice once begun of charging branch-line losses to capital instead of deducting them from income. So dividends, or perhaps bond interests, were paid year by year on alleged earnings of the main line, when in fact such earnings were annually overstated. The Louisville and Nashville Railroad just mentioned is an instance of this latter policy also : for in 1894 it began for the first time to deduct from its profit-and-loss statements the losses on one of its main branches which it had for years beeen carrying as " assets " in an optimistic hope that the amounts " advanced " to the branch would be made up from increased earnings. In that same year, 1894, the New York, Lake Erie, and Western began also for the first time to deduct the losses of its auxiliary companies from its main line income account. The policy of carrying branch-line deficits as assets in the general balance-sheet was carried out systematically by the Richmond and West Point Terminal Railway and Warehouse Company. Those who wish to follow the matter further will find abundant illustration in the records and reports of that company and of the railways embraced in its control. In this way "investments" in branch-line roads or other subsidiary property were increased on one side of the ledger, to be balanced by an equal increase of funded, floating, or current debts on the other. It was inevitable under such a system of accounting and of dividend paying that the real weakness of a system should be revealed at the first touch of adversity. It usually happens that the limit of credit to such a company comes at the very time when good credit is essential in order to tide affairs over a temporary decline in profits. No more money can be borrowed, for the borrowing powers have been exhausted in order to collect funds for past payments to bond- or stockholders ; a receivership then becomes unavoidable and the true state of things becomes publicly known.

A few systems, some only when really insolvent and some while solvent, have adopted the policy of charging off against surplus income the losses of auxiliary companies which had been accumulating perhaps for many years. Such housecleaning should be general. A healthy financial opinion regarding the wisdom of conservatism in estimating profits, is not the least of the good effects of business depression. Among systems which have pursued a rash course so long that the holdings of shares are endangered, it is useless to hold the accounting department responsible. As remarked, the process of debiting or crediting items to certain accounts on certain ledgers, is simple ; the real difficulty lies in putting a correct opinion upon the items themselves and in formulating a clear mercantile theory about them and that which they represent.

In a large number of cases the parent company, in order to create a market for branch-line bonds or to buy the control of certain independent roads, has guaranteed the payment of interest on these bonds as well as payment of the principal at maturity. In our corporation history there have been instances of the repudiation of such guaranties, and the question of their commercial value is raised in the reorganization of nearly every large system. The forms of words which contain this guaranty are many. " For value received " is perhaps the most common, the usual meaning of that phrase being that the traffic connection gives to the guaranteeing company an equivalent for its obligation. In certain cases the language means merely that the parent company agrees that the interest shall be paid to the bondholders ; it then sometimes happens that the obligating company purchases the coupons without cancelling them. By this method the lien of interest would not be discharged but kept alive ; and at the maturity of the mortgage these purchased coupons are legally entitled to rank with the bonds in claiming part of the property. An instance may be found in the history of the consolidation of the former roads into the Pittsburgh, Cincinnati, Chicago, and St. Louis Railway Company in 1890. The practical effect of such purchasing is to weaken the value of the bonds to that extent. The guaranteeing company, however, cannot " purchase " coupons, but must pay and cancel them unless there is express authority for the former course.

Other forms of guaranty recite certain specific considerations or refer back to certain conditions not given in the endorsement on the bond but contained in the resolutions of the Board of Directors and not easily accessible to the public. If the matter is of importance, it is advisable for all holders of guaranteed bonds to consider the form of guaranty carefully and to obtain and read the proceedings of the different boards of directors or officers or committees which have dealt with the subject. In this way a clear idea may be obtained of the nature of the obligation and of the consideration which has been given for that obligation.

The courts have always upheld and enforced the guaranties of railway companies whenever that was legally possible ; still, if a company resolves to repudiate its obligations, it will often find a legal reason for so doing. The laws governing such transaction in the several States are sometimes conflicting, and the question of the applicability of this or that statute or section of the constitution to a particular case is often so much in doubt that the question of lack of power to make such a contract or to enter into such a guaranty is easily raised if a company needs to do so ; and it is often hard to settle. The innocent holder of repudiated bonds is entitled to the benefit of every doubt and usually gets that benefit ; but, as before stated, if a company decides to dishonor its promises, the legal points it may raise are many, and the result not always clear. The repudiation by the Evansville and Terre Haute Company in 1894 of its guaranty on Evansville and Richmond bonds is in point. In estimating the value of guaranteed bonds, therefore, the holder must take into consideration the general reputation for good faith and solvency which the company bears in the opinion of the financial public.

There have been instances in our corporation experience in which companies have justified their repudiation of guaranties by a general argument. That argument usually runs thus : " A company has guaranteed the almost perpetual payment of certain interest. At the time such an agreement was made the circumstances justified the bargain ; the branch taken over was worth

to the main company all that was annually to be paid
for it.   But in a few years business changed greatly ;
another road was built into the branch's territory, or
the mine or manufacturing, for which the branch was
projected, gave out.   In fine, the yearly result to the
guaranteeing company is now a heavy deficit under the
agreed rental.   Should the company be kept to the
letter of its contract no matter what happens, or should
the branch share in the common loss ?   The equity of
a continuing contract is a thing yet commercially unde-
termined.   In business affairs most continuing contracts
which involve loss upon either party are settled either
by a compromise or by the insolvency of the losing
party.   In trade the instances are very few indeed
where such losses are paid regularly year by year
indefinitely.   It is true that for obvious reasons the
courts always insist upon the letter of a contract because
the sacredness of contracts is vital to business ; yet the
statement that no machinery exists for determining
such questions does not alter the fact that the common-
sense of mankind is against the enforcement of such
unfair contracts running indefinitely.   The principle is
the same as that which allows a debtor to escape his
debts under certain conditions, because it would be
hopeless and cruel to keep a man in jail or even in debt
for his whole life.   That no such rule exists for corporations merely shows that corporation law has not got
that far ; meanwhile suffering companies try to reach
precisely that end through legal quibbles and consider
themselves commercially entitled to carry their purpose
out if possible.''

Arguments like these have convinced a few thinkers,
and in consequence propositions are sometimes heard
that continuing guaranties should be made adjustable

as to percentage of returns every ten or twenty years.
The lease of the Central Pacific to the Southern
Pacific was so drawn. The argument of a defaulting
corporation is, however, usually weakened by the facts
of the case. A company wishes at the time to build a
new line or buy control of one already existing. The
situation is carefully considered by the officers and
directors and the degree of necessity decided upon.
That company must pay for that line, and must agree
with the money-lenders or the owners as to terms. If
it could borrow money on its guaranty at five per cent.,
let us say, but could not induce the capitalists to build
the line and take their chances without a guaranty at
less that ten per cent., let us suppose, then clearly
enough the five per cent. saved annually by guaranteeing the bonds is a part of the consideration though it
may not be mentioned in the documents ; the saving is
of the nature of an insurance given by managers who
ought to know what they are doing. If now the expectations of these managers be not realized, it is not simple equity to demand a readjustment. If that had been
the idea originally, the investors would have demanded
much higher returns at the start. Readjustments have
never been in commercial favor even when provided for
in contracts. The statistics are in the hands of one of
the parties, the other being able to get but slight
knowledge of the real facts. For these reasons capitalists have been unwilling to accept adjustable guaranties, considering them not so much inequitable as
uncertain and indefinite.

It follows from what has been said that guaranteed
bonds are often safe but sometimes not. It is a mistake
for investors to buy bonds merely because they are
guaranteed, and oftentimes a mistake in financiering

for companies to issue them expecting them to find
favor on that ground alone. The terms and conditions
under which the guaranty was given, the form in which
the obligation is set forth, the good faith of the guaranteeing company, are all to be carefully considered.
In some cases the replies to these questions will be so
satisfactory that no further investigation need be made,
especially if we believe the revenues of the company to
be equal to the fixed charges and something more ; for
the ability of a company to earn its interest is as important as its intention to pay if earned.

In a large number of cases it is well for the investor
to look a little further and for the company to ask him to
do so. The question in such an investigation is: Does
the guaranty represent the commercial situation ? Does
the branch line really earn the interest on its bonds ?
Is it as it stands worth to the guaranteeing company
all that it costs that company annually in interest and
expenses ? If so, the bonds are, for the time at least,
secure. This question is in a great many cases very
hard to determine. The same neglect which has been
discussed in previous pages of this chapter regarding
branch lines whose bonds are not guaranteed, follows
these guaranteed roads also. Many companies have
not kept these accounts so as to show whence their
revenues are really derived ; such companies ought to
suffer in credit for their carelessness. The financial
position of branch-line bonds, whether dependent upon
the traffic of the roads covered or upon the guaranty
of the main line, should be clearly defined. An opinion
as to the value of such branch-line bonds, guaranteed
or not, is then possible. The more favorable that
opinion, the better is it for the company which is
responsible for them.

CHAPTER V

CORPORATION ACCOUNTING

EVOLUTION in accounting is to be expected the same as in the methods of conducting business. As the transactions become numerous and increase in complexity, a corresponding change in the style of keeping the books is demanded. The principles of bookkeeping are simple, and the various kinds of entries are easy of general comprehension. The practical difficulty lies in making the books set forth the real facts ; for it is in judging of the true meaning of those facts that the statistician's art consists, the process of recording the figures, once the facts are agreed upon, being comparatively easy. Moreover, truth is many-sided ; a business optimist will see things favorably and make up his figures accordingly, while an ultra-conservative merchant will seek to have the position of his affairs set forth in the most unfavorable light. There is the more excuse for optimism in corporation matters, for corporations live on, and having more extended credit, often live down losses which would wreck partnerships ; thus it sometimes happens that for his own reputation's sake and because of that good credit, the manager of a large corporation will give to his statements the brightest colors that the circumstances permit. For these reasons criticisms upon corporation reports are so often unfavorable ; not because of malice on the part of the critic, so much as of abounding optimism on the part of the usual corporation manager. The excuse for such optimism should fairly be taken into account : that there is no hard-and-fast line between fact and credit ; that many a railway (for illustration) is helped over a bad place by its credit, and helped safely, whereas if the exact truth were known, that credit might be destroyed and with it perhaps the whole capitalization. A little unwilling forbearance on the part of creditors may bring everything around right and cause no loss.

Every corporation must adopt such forms of accounts as suit its particular business. They should embrace such a number of separate books as will enable the management to know exactly what is being done in every department and in every detail and at what cost. The collection of statistics costs money, but modern experience is showing that only by accurate statistical knowledge can modern business be successfully carried on. There are good systems containing elaborate provisions for ascertaining the various costs in manufacturing. A corporation should be more, rather than less, exact than a firm. The sources of profit down to the minutest detail should be carefully inquired into ; in no other way can the manager know which class of work to encourage, or which to study with a view of improving the process of production.

In large companies the main account is that of the general balance-sheet, in which are regularly stated the other accounts such as surplus income or profit and loss. Thus the balance sheet reflects merely the changes in the general condition during the year, not the amount of profit. This table or statement is the one upon which the lender of money or the investor should bestow his careful scrutiny, because on the interpretation of the items depends one's judgment as to the solvency of the company. The income table is simply an account of the earnings and expenses in totals, together with the proper deductions from the net revenue for the year. Accompanying the income account should be tables explaining in full detail the items there given in gross. There may be a difference of opinion between the managment and the bond- or shareholders as to the proper disposal of certain items of expenditure made during the year. There may be a legitimate question whether such items are properly chargeable to income or not ; such questions are not only theoretical but very practical, because on their answer often depends whether a dividend is paid or not. ˙ For such reasons the report which every corporation ought to make to its shareholders and the public (if the public holds the shares) should contain statements in sufficient detail of every transaction during the year, whether included in the income account or not, in order that every one may form his own judgment on the wisdom of the management and the safety of his investment.

In cases where the charging of items of expenditure to the income account may be a doubtful policy, or where, from the nature of the case, it is difficult to decide such questions, since the answer may depend upon one's opinions as to the business prospects for the future, the profit and loss account offers an easy compromise. To this profit and loss account may be credited annually all the surplus earnings of the corporation over and above fixed charges and dividends, or fixed charges only, leaving dividends for the profit and loss table. Against these surpluses may be charged from time to time the cost of unproductive improvements ; the deficits of subsidiary companies, which for the time must be met from the revenues of the owning corporation ; sums which have been included in the earnings of previous years and which have now proved uncollectible, and in general all items which, in the judgment of the management, should not be deducted from the income of the year, but which good financiering requires should be treated in the accounts in some way as debits, even if temporarily, in order that no inflation in the assets may occur. Such a profit and loss account, if carefully and fully kept, will prove a better test of the earning capacity of the company than the income account, which shows the profits in any one year, for the reason that the former table gives an average of results extending over a number of years. The annual reports of the Denver and Rio Grande Railway are worthy of study in this particular.

One of the perplexing things in the financial management of a large manufacturing or trading company, is the treatment of the expenditures for the care of the plant. A depreciation account in some shape must be kept by every company or firm in business. The real estate may decline in value, and in any case, in any progressing concern, money will be required to be spent each year to adjust the buildings more perfectly to the requirements of the business, and yet these adjustments may not add anything to the salable value of the property, and should not, therefore, be added in the accounts to the company's investment in real estate. In like manner, machinery will wear out, and is always subject to the danger of new inventions, which may render the old machinery practically worthless. It is not easy to foresee when a new outfit will be in part or in whole required, though experience soon places a limit to the number of years in which a given set of machinery may be useful. The proper course in these cases is always the conservative one. The corporation should estimate the probabilities of depreciation always against itself, and set aside yearly such sums from its profits as will suffice to renew so much of the plant as may be expected to wear out or to become useless in a given time. Unless this depreciation fund is carefully thought out and its separation from profits rigidly insisted upon, the shareholders of the corporation and perhaps the bondholders may in the course of years find that their securities cover a property of little or no business value. If certain sums · are not set aside to meet this depreciation, and if for this reason dividends are paid larger than would otherwise be the case, to the extent to which this is carried the returns received by the shareholders are not dividends but their capital returned to them in piecemeal. These depreciation sums should be real and not merely bookkeeping liabilities of the company to itself.

Modern corporation accounting requires that in theory a sharp line of distinction should be drawn between outlays which may be considered a part of the regular working expenses, and those which are chargeable to an increased investment in the business. In theory the former should be deducted from the gross earnings before the net revenue is determined, while the latter may be met by an increased issue of bonds or shares. There is no doubt of the correctness of this principle in general, but in its practical application it is subject to great modification. English shareholders in American corporations usually insist upon such a system of accounting as divides the expenditures strictly according to this rule ; and such indeed is the general practice in Great Britain. By charging to capital every item small and large which could by any possibility be construed to be a betterment, the British railways have increased their capitalization until they are dependent for a continuance of interest payments on good traffics year by year. Thus far no harm has come to these railways from this policy, because the fluctuations in the volume of their traffics have been comparatively slight.

But in the United States more caution must be observed in this matter. From the very nature of the case, business of all kinds in a developing country must be more subject to changes in profitableness than in older countries. The very character of the American people, energetic and progressive, makes business all the more liable to such fluctuations. Bad years follow good years in every line of American industry, although differences are less violent in those trades which are the longest established and among those companies which have been in operation long enough to render their business comparatively stable. The principle, therefore, of charging all so-called betterments to capital and meeting the cost from the sale of bonds or shares, requires modification according to the circumstances of each particular company. The more fluctuating the volume of business has been or is likely to be, the more important is it that in one form or another a part of the profits in prosperous years should be withheld from the shareholders and put into the property or set aside for its renewal. To those who wish a working principle to distinguish the proper items to be charged to capital account in the actual management of American corporations, railway and other, the following definition is suggested : No additions to the property

either to the real estate or to the machinery (if a manufacturing company), or to the roadbed and track (if a
railway company), should be considered betterments
and charged to capital, unless they increase the pro-
ductivity or earning capacity of the plant. Under this
rule the purchase of additional equipment for a railway
would be an expenditure which could conservatively be
met by the issue of bonds or equipment notes, because
such purchases would enable a larger volume of traffic
to be handled ; on the other hand, the replacement of a
wooden bridge by an iron one would not be a proper
charge to capital, under our definition, unless it was
one of a series of expenditures deliberately resolved
upon in order that heavier trains could be run and a
larger volume of traffic handled, thus increasing the
revenues of the company—an increase which our theory
demands should be clearly seen to be possible after the
various amounts of capital set aside for this purpose
had been spent. The same rule might be applied to
corporations other than railways ; the safe course is to
charge against revenues (possibly through the profit-
and-loss account) the cost of all additions to the property which do not increase the output or decrease the
cost of production. Yet any rule or any principle in so
delicate a matter can properly be applied in each case
only after a careful study of all the circumstances,
including the business of past years and the prospect
for the future. With railroad laws in nearly every
State permitting unrestricted building, American railroads are constantly liable to attack by competing lines
projected for legitimate or speculative purposes. In
England companies are not chartered unless a public
necessity for the proposed line is shown. In the United
States the only safe course for the old roads is to make

themselves strong by using a part of their earnings for betterments, thus keeping down the capital accounts. The Pennsylvania Railroad has pursued this policy for forty years, having in that time, according to its reports, paid eighty millions of dollars for betterments out of profits. The foreign shareholders have frequently complained of this policy, though experience has shown it to be an essential element in the present strength of that company.

On railways the working officers prefer to have included in the operating expenses only such sums as may rightly be grouped under that title. This is a proper request on the part of the superintendents, because they naturally wish that their administration of the affairs of the company should be shown to be conservative and careful. There is another reason also for keeping operating expenses distinct, in that it enables the managers to compare the same items of expenses year by year. If these items are varied by the inclusion or exclusion at times of sums whose proper accountings may be in doubt, the comparison of costs from year to year is vitiated and a valuable test of the efficiency of the operating officers is lost. To meet this requirement certain corporations deduct the costs of such betterments as one item from the net revenue often in the income statement. The objection to this course lies in the fact that the sums thus expended are lost sight of; and to the extent to which those items are hidden, the real amount of money spent upon the plant is understated. This is not a mere book-keeping objection. The railways have found that the real cost of their property is a factor in dealing with legislatures. Laws may be passed in order to reduce freight rates and passenger fares to a point which shall

yield the companies a return " on cost.." The same
point may arise at any moment with companies other
than railways. Every corporation should therefore so
keep its accounts as to show the amounts expended to
improve the plant year after year from earnings. A
common custom is to apply the annual surplus directly
to the construction charges for the year, bonds being
issued for the amount of the capital account after thus
deducting the surplus. That custom practically adds
the surpluses spent for betterments to the capitalization ; yet it is a question whether it would not be better
to open a comprehensive profit-and-loss account, in
which the cost of betterments, as well as other indirect
but necessary expenditures, could be included.

Corporations small in capitalization but public in
their nature and in their stock holdings, often conduct
businesses which do not require an elaborate system of
accounting. Such companies are often managed by
men who are themselves large owners in the property
and at the same time skilled in that particular trade.
Such men, for their own use or for that of the few other
shareholders, need only the simplest statements of the
business. It is customary in these small companies to
unite the general balance-sheet with the income account, and in their cases this custom leaves no difficulty. On the one side are stated the items of cost of
property, the valuation of the tools and machinery, the
cash in the bank, perhaps the amount of interest
charges and dividends paid during the year, and the
working expenses. On the other side of the account,
the revenues of the year, the bonded debt, and the
current debt. Such simple statements are well enough
for those who understand the business thoroughly,
while the changes in the items from year to year allow

of the working out of the various principles which
have just been discussed but about which no such
sharp distinction need be drawn as in the case of large
manufacturing companies. The original cost of the
property can be written off from time to time by adding
to the cash on hand a yearly sum before dividing
profits ; a method of keeping a depreciation account
which meets the peculiar requirements of such companies as have only a limited existence, such, for
instance, as those which operate a mine where the
amount of coal or ore can be estimated within reasonable limits. This sum of money in the bank is then
applicable to the extinguishment of the bonded or
share capital at the proper time, or may be used for
heavy improvements to the property if such should be
decided upon. Small corporations which have been
formed for family reasons, and whose shares are held
by the former partners and not sold to the public,
require no special discussion. Their affairs are managed very much the same as under the former partnership.

The formation and increasing numbers of corporations whose shares are held by the public and whose
business is trading, have led to a more rigid system of
estimating mercantile credits and of inspecting the
items upon which that credit is based. The evolution
of corporation (or partnership) credit is one which must
work for the good of all concerned. Such companies
yield increasing opportunities for the investment of
small sums, and while thus gathering together the little
rivulets of capital, their managers should themselves
be under a moral responsibility to take all the more
care of other people's money. It is well therefore that
the affairs of trading companies should be subjected to

such analyses as will indicate their solvency. Preparing statements that will stand examination is one of the best tests to which corporation managers submit as tending to bring the real position clearly before their own eyes and making them conservative in conducting the business and in estimating profits for the shareholders. Following this thought further, below will be found the statement of a non-existing trading company, whose assets and liabilities may be commented upon without reserve. The figures chosen for the purpose are intentionally doubtful and do not, of course, reflect the real position of our small corporations. They have been compiled in this form arbitrarily and for the sake of comment.

"The Blank Trading Company" we will suppose was incorporated for the purpose of importing and selling fancy goods. The statement below is assumed to have been made December 31st and the inventory to have been taken on the same day. The head office is in New York City, with branches in Boston and Chicago. The president of the company is interested in a retail store in Chicago, to whom the company sells goods. The statement of assets and liabilities of the company is as follows:

THE BLANK TRADING CO.

ASSETS

A.	Cash on hand	$ 600
B.	Cash in Consolidated and other banks	4 000
C.	Bills receivable (due from customers)	7 000
D.	" " (due from branches)	10 000
E.	Accounts receivable (due from customers)	63 000
G.	Merchandise (valued at cost)	170 000
H.	Real estate	27 000
J.	Machinery and fixtures	800
K.	Merchandise in bonded warehouses	37 600
		$320 000

LIABILITIES

P.	Capital stock { preferred	$50	000
	common	50	000
Q.	Bills payable for merchandise	47	000
R.	" " to banks	15	000
S.	" " for commercial notes sold	10	000
T.	Open accounts	109	000
V.	Deposits of employees	4	500
X.	Profit and loss	34	500

$320 000

Some additional facts are assumed. A portion of the merchandise in warehouses is subject to "trust receipts." There is a contingent liability (not shown in the statement) of $20,000 for endorsed bills receivable outstanding. About $12,000 of accounts and bills receivable is acknowledged to be past due. Sales the preceding year amounted to $350,000. Expenses of conducting the business were $60,000, and dividends of eight per cent. upon preferred and twelve per cent. upon common shares, calling for $10,000, were paid during the year.

First as to the items of the statement. Item A, cash on hand, needs no particular comment. It represents actual money in the hands of the company. In a few instances where deliberate fraud was intended this item has been manipulated. Sometimes the words "and cash items" have been added so that uncollectible bills or things of that character could, by a stretch of language, be included. In one instance, where a payment was soon to be made to creditors, a sum of money was borrowed from the bank and called "on hand," though the bank by understanding did not allow the cash to go from its possession, retaining it at interest over statement day. But such cases are rare. "Cash" has a recognized meaning, and is correctly accounted for by the vast majority of companies and firms. Item B, cash in bank, also means what it says, being funds of the company on deposit and subject to cheque ; as our company is a reputable one, there is nothing to cause doubt as to these items of cash, A and B.

Item C, customers' bills receivable is a small one. If it were necessary to examine into it closely, one ought to know something about the customers whose bills are held and the character of the obligation. Business methods have changed in recent years. It was at one time the general custom to settle all accounts by giving bills. Now, with the exception of a few trades, it is customary to keep running accounts, so that the jobber does not have his customers' due bills as evidences of money owing to him as much as formerly. Of course, an obligation signed by two known firms, though one be small, is better than single-name paper ; but such paper is no longer obtainable in quantities. In the present case the item is considered a good asset.

Item D, covering bills receivable due from branches, must be thrown out. Since the branches are parts of the main house their obligations are also obligations of the main house, and cannot in any way be called assets. The confusion sometimes brought into the matter of the relations between parent houses and their branches, or between the home office of a corporation and its subsidiary offices, is cleared up when we remember that for the general purpose of estimating upon the financial value of shares and bonds, the branches and the head office constitute but one concern. If juggling with figures or technical book keeping operations is indulged in, it is usually done to conceal annual losses or depreciation or else to make the reported condition seem better than the reality. In small trading companies the matter is usually more simple. Instances have been known where the head office, ignoring the real position of its branches, has asked for bills payable to cover only the book keeping debts due to the parent company. These bills in the names of the branch were endorsed by the manager and discounted at the bank, the proceeds, of course, making a surprisingly excellent showing in the annual statement. The indorsed bills were not included among the liabilities because not considered " direct " obligations. Of course, the exhibit thus made was not a correct statement of the company's real condition. Many trading firms and corporations habitually exclude from their public announcement all indirect obligations of endorsement on the ground that they become a proper charge only when not paid by the maker. This is true so far as the sheet itself is concerned, but the share- or bondholder who wishes to learn all the facts should know by a separate statement how large these indirect endorsed obligations are. If out of proportion, it then becomes important to inquire why they exist, and how far the makers are financially responsible. The matter of indirect debts which may become direct, is one which should have careful consideration in all corporation management. A manager willing to take advantage of book keeping technicalities may not speak of contracts which he has made for the purchase of supplies or machinery because dated ahead, and therefore not yet direct obligations ; but all such prospective debts must be known if a clear view of the future is desired. The Blank Trading Company acknowledge that they have a contingent liability amounting to $20,000.

Item E, accounts of customers, is a most important one in a trading company's statement, and one equally hard to value. Book accounts and merchandise are the main assets of firms and corporations doing a trading business. If, upon investigation, it is found that these two items can be considered really good assets, the company is justified in expecting credit. The first question to ask concerning accounts receivable is : Are they in proportion to the amount of business done and not in excess of the proportion of the same item among other houses in the same trade? In some trades these book accounts run fairly uniform throughout the year. In others they vary so as to show large amounts at one season with small sums at another ; in the latter case one may judge of the item partly by the date of the statement. In the particular line of trade which has been chosen for our illustration the amount of accounts receivable on the last day of the calendar year ought to be quite small, increasing in amount from the first of the year until the conditions are reversed by spring or early summer. Perhaps ten per cent. of the gross aggregate sales would be a fair proportion to expect for this item in the statement under our assumed conditions. It will be noticed that this item is, therefore, about twice what it ought to be. This fact of itself furnishes a reason for further investigation. It is, of course, possible, that these accounts are all good —possible, but not probable. One might inquire how much of these book accounts is over-due and is carried along by the company. If the proportion of over-due accounts in this item is at all heavy, it is an indication either that goods have been too freely sold to irresponsible parties on credit, or else that some misfortune, such as the loss of a staple crop, has fallen upon a certain section of the community in which a large quantity of The Blank Trading Company's goods have been sold ; a possibility always to be borne in mind when inquiring whether the credit risks are scattered or practically confined to one or two sections of the country ; to be sure not to be caught by any technical differences, one should ask how many of these accounts have been extended when due, which, of course, is another way of carrying them. If the company will make up a statement of the customers who are indebted, one may obtain their rating from a mercantile agency and see what the proportion is between their capitals as thus reported and the obligations in question. If a large part of these obligations figure out to be more than twenty-five per cent. of the capital of these customers, one may distrust the value of their accounts. In the present case, it is stated that the president of the company is interested in a retail store to whom the company sells goods. Technically we may expect that the company would not consider the account of this retail store as over-due, and yet it is possible that the swelling of this item beyond the limits customary in that particular line of trade may be owing to the credits granted to this particular store. Perhaps it is found that suspicions are in part confirmed, and that the excess of book accounts over the normal amount is really dead-wood carried by the company. One, therefore, in his estimate of values, may put down this item at about $30,000.

Item G, merchandise. It is so easy to accumulate old and unsalable merchandise that nothing but eternal vigilance can keep a firm free from that error. It is very difficult for the ordinary investigator to make up his mind regarding this item in the company's statements ; so much depends upon the business instinct with which the goods are selected and the judgment

with which the future of the particular trade is fore-
casted.   Another matter that one should know is, on
what basis the value of the goods has been arrived at.
In our table it is stated that the merchandise is "valued at cost," meaning cost to The Blank Trading
Company.   In these figures, therefore, is included the
manufacturer's profit, which again is affected by the
credit of the purchasing company.   The open accounts
due by this corporation are fairly heavy, and one may
reasonably conclude that the merchandise has not been
reduced in cost by any discounts for cash.   In short, it
is proper to refuse to accept this item at its face value
in estimation on the solvency of the company.

In judging of a firm's or corporation's solvency the
character of the goods dealt in must always be borne in
mind.   The difference between staple and fancy goods
is one which not only distinguishes one trade from another but is an important distinction many times to be
drawn between a certain set of articles and another in
the same store.   Groceries may be accepted at almost
full value even under the hammer, while silks and rib-
bons are dependent upon the caprices of fashion from
one season to another.   In like manner hardware can
be taken at a close estimate nearer to its inventory
value than can boots and shoes.   Wool is a more stable
article than woollens ; and so we might go through the
list.   In the present instance it is proper to say that
fancy goods are of uncertain value, yet one may assume
that The Blank Trading Company deals in the more
stable kinds.   Nevertheless, it is clear that one cannot
assume the full value for the stock of merchandise in
question if sold at auction.   Balancing all these probabilities, the value of this item may be fixed at $100,000.

The proper valuation to be put upon book accounts

and merchandise in cases of insolvency are constant subjects of study among those whose business it is to loan money to firms or companies either by direct discount or through purchase of commercial paper. Below is a table of liquidating values for five trades, compiled by a banker of experience :

Trades	Accounts Receivable percentage good	Merchandise percentage good
Hardware	72	80
Dry Goods	67	70
Boots and Shoes	80	65
Furniture	70	68
Groceries	40	95

The experience of different bankers and of different trading firms and companies may be more favorable or unfavorable than this table indicates regarding the realizable value of book accounts and stocks of merchandise. It should, therefore, be modified in accordance with the business reputation of the men in charge, or of the traders in the particular section to whom the goods have been sold on credit.

Item H, real estate, $27,000. This value seems a little high for the comparatively small amount of business done, and should have further investigation. Some small companies, sometimes through carelessness rather than actual error, add the cost of improvements made from year to year to the value of their real estate until this item comes to stand on their books at an amount much in excess of its actual selling worth. In the present instance, it is assumed that this has been the practice, and that the actual value of the property by appraisal is $15,000.

Item J, machinery and fixtures, is a small one in

7

any case and need not be commented upon. If it were
an important item, one should inquire as to the depreciation.

Item K, merchandise in bonded warehouses, $37,600,
is subject to the same criticism as regards its real value
as that already passed upon the merchandise in stock ;
that is, for the purpose of questioning the solvency of
the company or of putting a value upon its preferred or
common shares the figures named in the statement are
too high. In addition to this, it is noted in the business
statement that a part of this bonded merchandise is
subject to trust receipts.

It is a common practice for firms doing an importing
business to have the foreign goods consigned to a New
York City banking house, upon whom also the foreign
bills are drawn payable in a certain number of days,
varying according to the customs of the different countries. It frequently happens that these goods reach
their destination before the bills drawn against them
are due. In order that the merchandise may be sold
by the importing firm soon after arrival, an arrangement to this effect is made through trust receipts.
One form of such receipts gives the importing house
possession of the goods, but without title, the house or
corporation guaranteeing to hand the proceeds of the
sale over to the banking house. Another form permits
the putting of the goods in store under warehouse
receipts. These forms are varied according to the circumstances of the case and the credit and standing of
the importing company; but in whatever way the business is transacted, the meaning is that the merchandise
affected is not the property of the importing house,
and cannot, therefore, be included in its list of assets.
In the present case, something must be deducted from

this face value on this account also. It will be dealing generously with this item if it is put down at $20,000.

By adding up the assets as re-valued, we find the total to be $177,400. A glance at the table of liabilities shows a total of $320,000. If from this one deducts for his own purpose capital stock and the profit and loss—the latter item being simply to balance accounts, —he finds the actual debts for money to amount to $185,000, or about $8000 more than the assets as valued in our examination. This means, in effect, that if the company should be wound up, the holders of both preferred and common stock would lose their whole investment and very likely some of the creditors also would not be paid in full. Although according to the statements this trading company paid dividends last year amounting to eight per cent. upon the preferred and twelve per cent. upon the common shares, yet it is clear that no dividends ought to have been distributed until a fund had been accumulated which would balance the possible bad debts and depreciation of merchandise of which we have spoken.

The sales are stated to have amounted the preceding year to $350,000. This, it will be noted, is only 3½ times the capital. There has been some gross mismanagement of the business because modern conditions demand that the capital should be turned over many more times than this during the year. This impression is confirmed when we look at the amount of business expenses, $60,000. Taking the expenses and dividends together, it will be noticed that it required twenty per cent. profits on the small amount of sales to meet them. Few business houses in these days of sharp competition can be assured of the continuance of so large an average gross profit as that at wholesale. There is clearly something the matter with the affairs of the company. It is possible that some of the excess in accounts receivable already spoken of represents bad debts contracted by the company in order to cover so large an amount of business expenses. To secure so large a percentage of profit they have been willing to sell goods to retail houses with indifferent credit. If these bad debts had been charged off there would have been no dividends and it might have been found that expenses had not been earned.

Although the valuation put on the assets shows that at forced sale they would only realize enough to pay the creditors, it does not follow that the affairs of the company cannot be retrieved. There is a foundation here for better business. If energy and ability can be secured, in the management, the amount of sales can be doubled and expenses reduced so as to show a great change in the proportion to the volume of trade. If for a while the profits thus realized could be applied to the reduction of the uncertain items among the assets, it is possible that in a few years the aspect of things could be so completely changed as to show that the company was again in a sound condition.

Complete change in the modern methods of supplying mercantile credits makes it necessary for the lender of money whether on commercial paper or in the form of bonds or of preferred shares, to rely upon the general solvency of the firm or corporation. This of itself makes needful a more or less thorough investigation into the whole affairs of the borrowing houses. Very likely in this matter as in other lines of business there will arise banks and banking houses which will make a specialty of such loans.

The same set of facts puts a new responsibility upon

the firms and companies which ask for credit. These requests for loans involve two things : first, that the borrowers are honest and mean to pay—which, in the majority of cases, is taken for granted,—and second, that there is a reasonable hope of their ability to pay. This latter point does not concern the honesty of the managers, but depends for its answer upon a wide estimate of business facts. It is, therefore, no reflection upon a borrowing firm or company to have the investor or lender ask for such a statement of their affairs as shall enable him to form a business judgment upon their condition. The asking for investment money on mercantile loans from banker or investor implies, therefore, that such a statement shall be forthcoming.

The habit of making such statements for more or less public examination will cause the managers to give even closer attention to the meaning of various items which they are carrying upon their books. In this way conservatism is increased by the conditions of doing business, which now demand, on the one side, large loans of capital, and, on the other, business ability and honesty without sentimentalism.

CHAPTER VI

THE EXAMINATION OF RAILWAY REPORTS

THE bonds and shares of the railways of the United States form the most available investments or instruments of speculation for the people. The general knowledge about railways is greater and the industry itself more firmly established than is the case with other large enterprises. The securities of these railways are the ones most prominently dealt in upon our exchanges, thus giving to holders the important advantages of easy and quick purchases or sales. For these reasons it is advisable that the items which are contained in the usual annual reports should be analyzed at length and in detail, in order that any purchaser or holder may be able to form for himself a general idea of the meaning of railway statistics and of the importance of the differences appearing in those reports from year to year.

The Great Eastern Railway is a supposititious road in the United States east of the Missouri River. Having no actual existence, its supposed records can, without invidious comparisons, be made the text of an examination into the meaning of railway statistics, and the relation of one item to another in such tables as are usually printed in railway annual reports.

Although paying four per cent. dividends, it is assumed that the stock of the Great Eastern Railway is not quoted at very high prices on the exchanges. A company which is really earning four per cent., and which seems likely to continue earning and paying that dividend, usually finds its stock well thought of in financial circles. Contrary to this rule, a holder of Great Eastern shares sees his stock declining under daily sales presumably by "insiders." Naturally his attention is aroused ; he asks himself why the prices of his shares should fall ; in search of information which should satisfy his questionings, he first takes up the annual report of his railway and looks over the figures given therein. On the first pages he finds an income account for the last fiscal year, containing nothing which on the face of it could be construed unfavorably. The statement of the result of the year is as follows :

GREAT EASTERN RAILWAY : INCOME ACCOUNT

TO JUNE 30

Gross earnings :	passenger	$1,080 000
	freight	5,600 000
	mail and express	120 000
	Total	6,800 000
Operating expenses (62 per cent.)		4,200 000
Net earnings		2,600 000
Add interest on bonds owned		250 000
Gross income		2,850 000
Fixed charges : taxes............ $100 000		
bond interest.... 1,300 000		1,400 000
Net income		1,450 000
Dividends at four per cent		1,200 000
Surplus for the year, carried to profit and loss		250 000

On succeeding pages of the annual report are given the results for the year of the Rich Valley Railroad, a branch or feeding line, owned by the Great Eastern Company, but operated independently :

Gross earnings....................................	$1,500 000
Operating expenses..............................	1,400 000
Net earnings....................................	100 000
Guaranteed bond interest paid....................	700 000
Deficit for the year.............................	600 000

There is nothing which necessarily shows bad management in the fact that a " feeder " is not self-supporting. The Rich Valley, as its name implies, may be a short line running through a rich agricultural and manufacturing district, the greater part of whose traffic is carried by the parent road to the great markets. Were it not for this branch the traffic would seek a rival road. Hence in this case the profits resulting from the carriage of this extra business are worth to the Great Eastern Railway, it is assumed, a great deal more than the $600,000 which it loses through its guaranty of Rich Valley bonds. The policy of building or purchasing branch lines which are run at a loss may, of course, be carried to such an extreme as to involve the guaranteeing company ; particularly when the real effect of such annual losses is concealed by the method of book-keeping adopted in this case. Clearly the Great Eastern Company must pay this deficit of $600,000 ; but from what fund ? Since the gross and net earnings of the main line receive all the benefit of the traffic turned over to it by the branch, and since, as we have assumed, this benefit is great, it follows that the cost of procuring that extra traffic is a proper charge against the income helped thereby. In other words, the annual loss of $600,000 on the branch line, unless clearly but a temporary deficit, ought to be deducted from the gross income of the Great Eastern Railway before a dividend is declared. If this is not done—and a glance back at the income account presented shows no mention of the item,—the real earning power of the company is to that extent overstated and the dividend unjustifiable.

How, then, is the deficit of the Rich Valley branch carried ? To answer this question the general balance-sheets for two years must be examined. These general balances show on the one side the assets of the company and on the other the liabilities. The different amounts are stated at their face and not at their intrinsic values. Ordinarily it is useless labor to go through a company's general balances for the sake of getting at the actual worth of the properties. Hence, for the information of ordinary shareholders, the most important object in having general balance accounts is the opportunity afforded for annual comparison. If we note the changes in the items from one year to another, we can often get valuable hints about the real prosperity of the company, because the facts thus revealed may not be mentioned in the text of the annual report. First, then, should be stated the balance-sheet for two years :

GREAT EASTERN RAILWAY

GENERAL BALANCE-SHEET, JUNE 30, PREVIOUS YEAR

Assets		Liabilities	
Cost of road......	$45,000 000	Capital stock.....	$30,000 000
Cost of equipment	10,000 000	Funded debt (5 %),	25,000 000
Stocks owned,		Interest accrued..	500 000
Rich Valley Co.	1,000 000	Due connecting	
Five per cent.		roads	600 000
bonds of Rich		Due for wages....	500 000
Valley branch		Supply accounts	
owned.........	5,000 000	payable.......	100 000
Advances to Rich.		Claim vouchers	
Valley........	400 000	audited	100 000
Due from connect-		Profit and loss....	5,500 000
ing roads......	250 000		
Materials on hand,	200 000		
Accounts receiv-			
able	100 000		
Suspense accounts	100 000		
Cash on hand....	250 000		
	$62,300 000		$62,300 000

GREAT EASTERN RAILWAY

GENERAL BALANCE-SHEET JUNE 30, PRESENT FISCAL YEAR

(Corresponding to the income account given above.)

Cost of road......	$48,000 000	Capital stock.....	$30,000 000
Cost of equipment	11,000 000	Funded debt (5 %).	27,000 000
Stocks owned,		Interest accrued..	700 000
Rich Valley		Due connecting	
branch........	5,000 000	roads	1,000 000
Advances to Rich		Due for wages ...	700 000
Valley........	1,000 000	Accounts payable,	300 000
Due from connect-		Bills payable.....	1,000 000
ing roads......	200 000	Supply accounts	
Materials on hand	150 000	payable	300 000
Accounts receiv-		Claim vouchers	
able	300 000	audited........	200 000
Suspense accounts	200 000	Profit and loss....	5,750 000
Cash and cash			
items	100 000		
	$66,950 000		$66,950 000

A brief explanation of the items first may be desirable. The costs of road and equipment are approximate statements of the amount of money spent for these objects, though they contain items which are only indirectly a charge against cost. For example, in those balance-sheets will be noticed an increase of bonds from $25,000,000 to $27,000,000 during the year. If these bonds were sold at a discount, say twenty per cent., the amount so deducted from their face value, $400,000, would not represent money put into the road directly or physically, though the whole increase, $2,000,000, it will be noticed, is added to cost of road in another way, *i. e.*, in its lack of credit. Sometimes this item of bond discount does not arise from lack of credit but from an attempt to issue bonds at a rate of interest so low, compared with the ruling rate in the money market, that par cannot be obtained for the bonds. In such cases, since the income account presumably is benefited by the small annual interest charges, that same income account should be debited each year with a proportion of the loss by the discount. The item profit and loss has misled many. If the assets foot up more than the liabilities (and every road tries to have it so, even as a matter of book-keeping, for appearance's sake), the item appears on the liability of the account. It will thus be seen to be what it really is, merely the balance between the assets and liabilities in the general balance-sheet representing the supposed excess of property over the capitalization and debts. It is not money in hand : it usually covers former annual surpluses which may long ago have been spent for equipment or on road, or invested in the materials carried in the storehouses and not yet put into the property. If a road has cash or salable securities in unusual measure, these will be found on the opposite side of the accounts as assets.

Another item is the interest accrued but not due. Such accrued interest should always be put down as a liability in balance-sheets, otherwise an unreal prosperity would be shown at one time or an unreal depression at another, according as the bond interest becomes payable. In all railway tables there are found items of current accounts with connecting roads both debit and credit, cost of materials and supplies purchased but not yet used or charged to the respective operating departments, and the like, being things for which working capital must be provided. Two further items in our statements merit notice. Supply bills payable is one. Every report should be examined to see whether this liability is included. It is the custom for all large companies to buy their fuel, rails, ties, etc., on time. Hence every company on any particular date has a large amount of obligations out, which are not yet due and for which no notes have been issued. Technically these may not be considered in the balance-sheets until due, but since they are sure to become due shortly, there can be no true statement of the company's condition made without including them. Sometimes when engines and cars have just been purchased, these unrecorded obligations may be very heavy. Again, when in straits for money, railway companies do not hesitate to pigeon-hole the bills for supplies sent them until the accumulated debts become large ; and, if not stated in the balance-sheets, an untrue appearance of ease in money matters is given.

Audited vouchers often form a growing obligation when traffic is depressed. Claims for losses of goods and rebates (not always unfair) are common ; in spite of care, overcharges in the freight bills rendered consignees will be made through the errors of clerks; wrecks may destroy much property for which the company is responsible; cattle may be hurt by trains; and, worst of all, accidents may kill or maim passengers. The claims thus presented to the company are often very large in amount. After investigation a certain portion are pronounced true claims and marked for payment. Such items are called "audited claims or vouchers" and should find a place in every balance-sheet. The still larger amounts of claims for losses, overcharges, or rebates not yet passed upon cannot well be stated in the balance-sheet, because their amount is uncertain, yet when "cut rates" are freely given the aggregate of claims and rebates which must presumably one day be paid may be so great that the amount, if known, would make a serious impression. Yet, on the other hand, where the sum of such unaudited claims stays approximately the same from year to year, no real harm is done by not attempting to include them in the company's tables.

Among the assets the items "accounts receivable" and "suspense accounts" require little explanation. These are claims carried by the company against other roads or against merchants. They may be good or they may not. Every company should have a separate table of "Profit and Loss," to which all such doubtful credits should be charged. It may be technically correct book-keeping to keep uncollectible accounts standing among the assets of the general balance-sheet, but no matter how the rules of book-keeping treatises may read, the object of all corporation accounting is to represent the commercial facts.

Companies which hesitate to deduct losses (branch-

line losses included) from their income account and yet
shrink from actually calling such losses "assets" should
charge such deferred claims to " Profit and Loss,"
crediting that account with the annual surpluses from
operation. The difference would then show the real
earnings. If at any time such old claims should become collectible, the same account could be credited
with the sums thus recovered.

The array of figures in our general balance-sheets
looks a little bewildering ; so to make the matter
clearer, we will tabulate the changes during the year :

EXPENDITURES :

FOR WHAT PURPOSE INCURRED

Increase in cost of road	$3,000 000
" " cost of equipment	1,000 000
" " advances to Rich Valley	600 000
" " accounts receivable	200 000
" " suspense accounts	100 000
	$4,900 000

RESOURCES :

WHENCE DERIVED

Decrease in amounts due from connecting roads	50 000
" " material on hand	50 000
" " cash and cash items	150 000
Increase in funded debt	2,000 000
" " interest due	200 000
" " amounts due connecting roads	400 000
" " wages due	200 000
" " unadjusted accounts	300 000
" " bills payable	1,000 000
" " supply accounts due	200 000
" " vouchers audited	100 000
" " profit and loss	250 000
	$4,900 000

This summary of changes in the position of the company during the year is worth study. The words "expenditures" and "resources" are used in their book-keeping sense : a decrease in the amount due *from* other roads and an increase in the amount due *to* other roads being both alike resources for our present purpose. The statement shows an increase in investment in road and equipment amounting to $4,000,000, of which more hereafter. The deficit of the Rich Valley branch is seen to have been carried in the accounts also as an increase in value of plant, offset on the other side of the account by money newly borrowed. We are assuming that this is not a correct principle and that the value of the property has not been advanced a penny through the Rich Valley, since all the profit for the branch for the year has already been included in Great Eastern earnings. This system of disposing of branch-line losses in the accounts is resorted to mainly to allow of borrowing money to meet the deficiency. Carrying subsidiary losses as assets and borrowing money or issuing bonds therefor, has been a common practice. The combination of many small roads into a large system permits such accounting, either through mistakes, optimism, or for purposes of deception, without danger of detection by superficial examination. Sometimes this way of concealing deficits is practised for a year or two during hard times, the officers intending to apply the surplus revenues of succeeding prosperous years toward wiping out all these imaginary assets and the debts contracted to pay for them. Such a policy should be leniently judged, if honestly held. Of course it is also proper to treat in this way a genuine loan when repayment is reasonably certain. The balance-sheets further show that the only bonds owned

by the Great Eastern Railway are those of the Rich
Valley branch.   A glance at the income account
shows $250,000 received from this source.   It thus
appears that in order to show that dividends had been
earned, the directors of the Great Eastern Company
did not charge up the losses of the Rich Valley branch
as they should have done, but did take credit to themselves for $250,000 unearned interest on their own
guaranteed bonds.

We now begin to grow suspicious and scrutinize the
items more closely.   The bonded debt and the bills
payable amount to $28,000,000, for which interest at
but five per cent. on the total (and money is not
always borrowed " in the street " at as low a rate as
that) would amount to $1,400,000 per year, whereas
but $1,300,000 is allowed in the income account.   This
may be an accurate statement for that particular table,
since the bonds may not have been issued for the
whole year and hence a year's interest may not yet be
due ; still our comparison shows that at least $100,000
must be added in our calculations to the requirements
for another year.

The expenditures in the table show $3,000,000 spent
upon the property and $1,000,000 upon equipment
during the year ; the other items make up a total expenditure of $4,900,000.   Let us now see how this sum
was obtained.   Allowing for the discount, $2,000,000
was raised from the sale of bonds and $1,000,000 was
borrowed on call (*i. e.*, can be demanded by the lender
at any time), or for a definite (though short) period.
The remaining $1,900,000 was gathered by piecemeal.
Debts due the company were more closely collected,
and on debts due by the company, it will be seen, payments were deferred.   Wages are running farther in

arrears and $200,000 more of bond interest was not paid. There is a new item " unadjusted accounts," which in this table undoubtedly is simply another name for more floating debt. Money due for supplies and for acknowledged claims has been held back. There has been further economy in the already too small stock of materials on hand. Cash is dwindling ; let the reader note the significant change in the wording of this item. A year ago it was " cash," now it is " cash and cash items." While " cash " has a definite meaning in Wall Street, the phrase " cash items " may cover a lot of rubbish which cannot be turned into cash at all—notes of bankrupts, disputed balances, and the like. It is not a harsh judgment which in this case assumes the amount of actual money on hand to be very small. Then the two offsets, accounts receivable and suspense accounts, down in the table as new assets worth $300,000, may fairly be rejected as assets altogether. A company in the position of the Great Eastern would not allow such accounts to be so much increased ; for being in stress for money it presumably would have collected them if they had been good.

The table of changes certainly wears a very unfavorable aspect ; yet one purpose of the managers has been accomplished, to cover up among a number of items a part of the money they have spent. Reliance is put on the fact that stockholders will not figure through the accounts.

Now as to the $4,000,000 increase in cost of road and equipment. Every report should contain a table giving in detail the items charged to construction or capital account. There is such a field for deception or for equally ruinous bad judgment in construction statistics

8

that the utmost publicity should be insisted upon. The following construction account is divided (arbitrarily as to these figures) into columns of proper and improper charges to capital.

CONSTRUCTION ACCOUNT

CHARGED TO CAPITAL

	Properly.	Improperly.
Road, for new rails..................	$400 000	
for damages from wrecks by accidents		$350 000
for renewals of ties............		150 000
for double track..............	700 000	
for new bridges..............	100 000	
for real estate bought..........	750 000	
for new stations..............	150 000	
Total charged to road, $3,000 000.		
Equipment, for 15 replaced engines...		150 000
for 15 new engines......	150 000	
for 500 replaced freight cars...................		250 000
for 500 new freight......	250 000	
for 25 replaced passenger coaches		100 000
for 25 new passenger coaches	100 000	
Total equipment, $1,000 000.		
	$2,600 000	$1,000 000

Every active concern must in some shape keep a depreciation account, to which shall be charged certain sums for renewal of machinery, etc., before profits are divided. If this is not done, the company will at the end find itself without plant and without money. In railway matters this is best accomplished simply by replacing cars and locomotives as they become worn out, and charging directly to operating expenses the cost of such new cars as do not add to the number of cars in use. In this way the quantity and quality of equipment or buildings or track are kept up at the expense of the annual earnings. In the construction account just given, $1,000,000 is improperly charged to capital and paid for by bonds, because the items cover depreciation and should have been included in the operating expenses. The test to be applied for the ascertainment of wrong charges to capital on equipment account is that of comparison. Every railway report gives, or should give, a list of the number of engines, passenger and freight cars in service at the close of the fiscal year. It is an easy matter to calculate the increases from year to year. For the reason that variations may at times occur, it is better to take a period of years. If the increases in the lists for, say, five years, multiplied by a fair valuation for each class, equal approximately the sums of the amounts charged to capital for new equipment during that period, then no wrong charges on this account have been made. In the case before us, we will compare the lists on two successive years.

STATEMENT OF EQUIPMENT

	Preceding year.	Present year.	Increase.
No. of locomotives	185	200	15
" " passenger cars	375	400	25
" " freight cars	29,500	30,000	500

This statement of equipment explains why, in the table of construction just given, $500,000 charged for replaced engines and cars is marked as improperly debited to that account. The actual increase in the list during the year is but half that carried in the company's balance-sheet as cost of plant. Other items included in the construction table as improperly charged, are payments for train accidents and for replaced ties. These, of course, should go into operating expenses. Payments for wrecks may, however, be concealed under " double-track " or similar items if a company is determined to deceive. As to ties, it is fair to assume that these last about seven years, depending, of course, on the climate and the kind of wood used. If we estimate 2800 ties to the mile of single track as about the average requirement, we have as an estimate of yearly renewals 400 ties per mile. Here, again, a number of years should be taken to obtain a fair average ; but, in the long run, if a road's renewals of ties fall on the average much below 400 ties per mile per year, inquiry should be made as to the reason.

As to rails : the life of a steel rail is not yet definitely ascertained ; perhaps twenty or twenty-five years may be taken in order not to be unfair to the company under examination. Estimating the weight of steel rails at seventy pounds per yard, the required weight per mile of single track is one hundred and ten tons. This would assume an average renewal of five or six tons per mile per year. A calculation spread over a number of years would show how far short of such an average a particular company had fallen. If its rails are new, or nearly so, such a calculation would be of value only as approximating the amount which will be required for that purpose in the future.

By our analysis of the Great Eastern's construction

account we have ascertained the amount which should have been charged to operating expenses, to have been $1,000,000. This added to the $600,000 loss on the branch line, makes $1,600,000 which should have been deducted from income. As the sum applicable to dividends in the income account was $1,500,000, we reach the conclusion that the dividend was not really earned and should not have been declared.

It will be remembered that the road was operated for sixty-two per cent. The percentage of expenses to earnings is of little use except as a guide for further examination. Of itself it is only the percentage relation between two sets of independent figures. If a railway earns one dollar and spends fifty cents, it is operated for fifty per cent. ; but if from any cause—water competition, let us say—it can get but seventy-five cents for the same unit of service, and if its expenses per unit stay at fifty cents, then it is operated for 66⅔ per cent. Usually the volume of units of traffic increases as the charge per unit falls, so that the road makes as much gross profit from the larger as from the smaller receipts per unit ; but manifestly we must go into details of the operating expenses if we would form a judgment upon the management. Here are four statistical tables of the Great Eastern Railway :

OPERATING EXPENSES

Maintenance of way and structures...............		$ 420 000
Maintenance of equipment :		
Passenger cars.............	$100 000	
Freight cars..............	300 000	
Engines..................	60 000	460 000
Conducting transportation.....................		2,320 000
General expenses................................		1,000 000
		$4,200 000

STATISTICS OF OPERATIONS

MILES OF RAILWAY OPERATED 800

Passenger-train mileage 1,800 000
Freight-train mileage.......................... 3,200 000
Switching, etc., mileage...................... 1,000 000
Total engine mileage.......................... 6,000 000
Number of passengers.......................... 800 000
     "   "   "   1 mile.................... 36,000 000
Tons of freight................................. 3,000 000
  " "   "   1 mile......................... 700,000 000
Rate of fare per mile, in cents.................. .03
Rate of freight per ton per mile, in cents........ .008
Mileage of passenger and baggage cars.......... 9,000 000
Mileage of freight cars........................ 96,000 000

GENERAL ITEMS

Maintenance of way per mile............... $525
Average number of passengers to each train mile.......... 20
Average number of tons to each freight train mile......... 220
Average number of passenger cars to each train........... 5
Number of freight cars to each train..................... 30
Average mileage of each freight car per day.............. 10
Average earnings per mile :
        each passenger train....................... $0.60
        each freight train......................... 1.75
Cost of motive power per engine mile :
        Repair of engines................. $0.01
        fuel............................... .05
        Engineers and firemen............. .07
        Oil and waste..................... .01 $0.14

Railway reports do not always give just these statistics, but usually the information we need can be obtained by a little figuring. The cost of maintenance
of way per mile is easily ascertained by dividing the
average number of miles operated into the total pay-

ments for that account. The average number of passengers or of tons of freight to each train is found by dividing the train mileage into the number of miles travelled by passengers or the tons one mile, respectively. The results are, therefore, somewhat in the abstract, but they afford the best comparison regarding the economy of the train service, one of the most important things to be considered in judging railway properties. It is necessary to know the number of miles run annually by cars, freight cars especially, in order that we may check the construction account and judge of the general efficiency of the company's management.

The amount allowed for maintenance of way is too small for the volume of traffic and number of trains. The sum varies from $2000 per mile in the case of our principal roads, downwards. Generally this item is best judged by comparing the amounts spent per year for a number of years with those spent by neighboring companies similarly situated. On many railroads the average annual cost of necessary repairs and renewals is $500 on each passenger coach, $40 each for freight cars, and $1000 each for engines. Multiplying these averages into the list of equipment given above, we find that there should be an addition of over a million dollars to the sum allowed in the operating expenses for repairs and replacement of equipment. This, of course, would increase the total expenses by that amount and correspondingly decrease the net income. As we know that the Great Eastern Railway (or any railway) cannot long be run without making the repairs and renewals its neighbors find necessary, we are forced to the conclusion that if money enough to care rightly for the property has been expended and charged to current working expenses, the fixed charges might not have been earned. Bankruptcy, therefore, awaits the company, unless heroic measures are taken to remedy defects in management and save the property. The decline in the market prices of the stock was more than warranted. Our inquiring stockholder would do well to dispose of his holdings at once at whatever price he can get ; unless his ownership is so large and his knowledge of railway operation so good as to enable him to ascertain and himself apply the proper remedy.

We have not yet exhausted comment on these tables. The cost of fuel (five cents per engine mile) is not high ; and if we add two or three cents to the cost of repairs for locomotives, the cost of motive power, per mile run, is low,—a point much in the company's favor. The rate received per ton per mile is not high, and perhaps a careful examination of the commercial conditions of the country through which the road runs would show where improvement is possible. The passenger department is grossly mismanaged. So many trains are run that the average number of passengers is only twenty per train mile. The average for the whole United States is about forty-five, and to carry less than thirty-five passengers per average mile is hardly profitable. Trains should at once be withdrawn until only the reasonable demands of the public are met. Since only half the present number of passenger cars is really needed, it was a gross abuse of power for the management to purchase more coaches, as the construction account shows they did. There is no particular fault to be found with the lading of the average freight train or with the earnings per freight train mile ; they are up to the average, if not beyond it. But to what use so many freight cars can be put is a mystery. It appears that the average mileage of the freight cars is but ten miles per day ; it should be at least three times that number to be profitable. The daily mileage of each freight car on the average is found by dividing the total freight-car mileage by the number of cars. Nine or ten thousand miles per year is the expected work of each freight car on the average on a successful road. Very likely more than half of the large number of cars owned (large in proportion to traffic carried) are standing idle on side tracks. The construction account showed 1000 cars bought at an expense of $500,000. Not a single car should have been added to the list, since under good management one third the number already owned should carry the stated volume of business. The extra number of cars should be reduced or loaned out to other roads, to be paid for at the standard rate for use of foreign cars, about three fourths of a cent per mile run. It sometimes happens that an unscrupulous company will charge renewals of equipment to capital and conceal the fact by adding the new cars to the old list of a year ago, even though it may not have in service the number of locomotives and cars certified to in the report ; such unjustifiable additions are called " vacant numbers." Vacant numbers sometimes arise from the destruction of worthless cars which should be replaced from operating expenses but temporarily are not, because of hard times. This is a legitimate economy if so stated in the report ; though it is better to charge against income the estimated cost of filling the vacant numbers. If the mileage of freight cars is stated in the report, these juggles with equipment, when at all serious, can be detected. If the company is really short of cars the cost of hiring equipment (itemized in the detailed table of operating expenses) will be a large and increasing sum. If more cars are, for the purposes of deception, kept in the lists than are actually running, either because old cars have been broken up and not replaced or are allowed to stand in the yards though worthless, the fact will be revealed by dividing the number of cars into the total mileage. If this total mileage includes foreign cars, such foreign mileage must be deducted and the mileage of home cars on foreign roads added. If, as in the Great Eastern case, the whole freight equipment ran an average of but 3200 miles during the year, when the average should have been 9000 miles or more, there is serious mismanagement or fraud. There has therefore been gross mismanagement or fraud also in locking up capital by the purchase of unnecessary equipment, which when bought must be kept in repair though perhaps falling to pieces through lack of use. In view of these latter criticisms it is probable that all the items in the construction account should receive careful investigation. The amount allotted to general expenses on a road carrying a fair amount of traffic should be not much over ten per cent. of the total expenses. Judged by this test the Great Eastern managers may be wasting about $500,000 a year. In short, the directors of this company are either " working " the road for their own benefit, or are culpably negligent of their duties as trustees for the stockholders.

It is often of importance to find out whether a company has much ready cash or is likely to be obliged to borrow for interest or dividends. An estimate upon this point is possible. Taking the balance-sheet given for the last fiscal year of the Great Eastern Railway on a former page, we find the cash items as follows :

Quick assets.		Quick liabilities.	
Due from connecting roads.......	$200 000	Due connecting roads............	$1,000 000
Accounts receivable...........	300 000	Due for wages....	700 000
Suspense accounts	200 000	Unadjusted accts..	300 000
Cash and cash items	100 000	Bills payable......	1,000 000
		Supply accts......	300 000
	$800 000	Vouchers	200 000
Excess of debts....	2,700 000		$3,500 000

Very likely the true state is a little worse than this, for while " unadjusted " or " suspense " debts must usually be paid in full at some time, accounts receivable or in suspense often cover items carried along in this way from year to year, and in part at least worthless or unavailable. The real cash resources as indicated in the above statement may be fairly set down as not more than half the sum stated, or $400,000. The item of accrued interest ought also to be included in the pressing debts, if the actual day of payment is near at hand—as, for example, July 1st, when the fiscal year closes June 30th. Materials and supplies, properly carried in the balance-sheet as assets since the company's working capital is invested therein, are not available for the payment of current debt and are therefore excluded from our table. A glance at the balance-sheet shows that the only treasury assets which can be sold are the bonds of the Rich Valley branch, amounting to $5,000,000. It is doubtful under our showing whether these bonds could be sold at a heavy sacrifice, if at all ; for an investigation would reveal the fact that the bonds were really dependent for their value upon the success of the system, since the branch line itself is not earning the interest. A proper inquiry at this point would be whether the Rich Valley is commercially entitled to a larger proportion of the combined earnings ; if so, its bonds would be enhanced in value, though the enhancement would be at the expense of the earnings of the main line.

Of course, the selling of Rich Valley bonds in the Great Eastern treasury would only exchange one form of debt for another, and would not therefore relieve the real situation. The company's affairs require thorough overhauling. Yet the fact that a company in temporary difficulties has in its treasury bonds available for sale, is often important. The obligation is changed from a floating to a funded debt, and therefore relieves the company from the fear of a receivership. Yet such a change really avails nothing in the long run unless the business or the management changes with it in such a way as to insure a greater success. The affairs of the company look desperate ; it is doubtful whether such an entanglement could be straightened out without a receivership for a few years, long enough to enable the pressing debts to be liquidated without too much sacrifice of the company's assets. Nevertheless, we see that in spite of gross mismanagement there is a good traffic, which in capable hands could be made to earn a fair revenue. We will, therefore, assume that indignant shareholders turn out the board of directors and discharge the officers, substituting capable and honest men. Let us suppose new directors and officers in charge. Of course the payment of dividends is suspended and all energies are devoted to saving the property from foreclosure. In such large affairs, all that is wrong cannot be righted at once. Corporate salvation is a work of time. In the present case we will assume that money could be borrowed to meet pressing needs, that two or three years' hard work has had its results, and that the income of the road is now meeting in full all proper operating expenses and fixed charges. Under these conditions the income account would be as follows :

Gross earnings: passenger......................		$2,000 000
freight.........................		7,000 000
mail, express, and miscellaneous.		600 000
Total earnings..............		9,600 000
Operating expenses (70 per cent.)		6,745 000
Total income...............		2,855 000
Fixed charges : taxes..................	$150 000	
bond interest..........	1,500 000	1,650 000
Net income.....................................		1,205 000
Deduct loss on Rich Valley bonds outstanding....	$350 000	
Deduct amounts set aside to pay interest and principal of old floating debts...	350 000	700 000
Surplus for year, devoted to improvements and betterments..............................		$505 000

This is very satisfactory. Passenger earnings have increased by the judicious issue of commutation and excursion tickets, though the fare received on the average has fallen from three cents to two cents per mile. In the intervening years the new officers have increased the volume of traffic. Taxes and bond interest have increased, and the losses on the Rich Valley branch are now properly charged. Evidently also the new management has adopted the policy of paying off old debts by degrees, $350,000 being set aside for that purpose. There still remains a surplus of $500,000, which is to be spent for improvements on the property.

Altogether there is a fair prospect of resuming dividends, so that those who purchased the stock when at its lowest point will very likely make large profits.

For the sake of contrast, the details of the operating expenses are given :

Maintenance of way			$1,000 000
Maintenance of equipment :			
	400 passenger cars at $500	$200 000	
	15,000 freight cars at $50	750 000	
	200 engines at $1000	200 000	1,150 000
Conducting transportation			4,095 000
General expenses			500 000
			$6,745 000

STATISTICS

Miles of railway operated, 800.

Passenger-train mileage	2,500 000
Freight-train "	3,600 000
Switching "	1,200 000
	7,300 000
No. of passengers, one mile	100,000 000
Tons of freight, one mile	900,000 000
Rate of fare in cents per mile	.02
" " freight " " "	.008
Mileage of passenger and baggage cars	12,000 000
" " freight cars	150,000 000
No. of passengers to each train	40
No. of tons of freight to each train	250

A generous amount is allowed for maintenance ; when the plant is once in excellent condition, it can be maintained at a less cost than that here given. The expense for trains earning revenue (this phrase excludes switching mileage and the like) is about $1 per train mile. In actual operation, this expense runs from eighty cents upwards per mile run, varying according to conditions, particularly the relative cheapness or dearness of coal, which forms a large item in all railroad expenses. As we have assumed that the Great Eastern Railway obtains its fuel cheaply, the assumed cost per train mile is fair, indicating reasonably high expenses for improving the property if the management is good, or a waste of money if the management is bad. Under the old state of affairs on this railway, the expense per train mile was about eighty cents. Our examination of details showed that this old appearance of cheapness was deceptive. Whether the new cost of about $1 per train mile is due to a generous care of the property or to greater waste, can be told only by further scrutiny into the accounts.

The table of statistics enables us to judge of the new management, and by contrast with the old figures shows important differences. The number of locomotives and passenger cars is the same as before. These have been presumably kept in good condition, the amounts allowed in the new operating estimates being fairly large. Freight cars have been reduced one half, partly by sale and partly by the breaking up of old and small cars which were uneconomical to use. The new management had to do the best they could with the property as they found it when coming into power. The number of passengers per train has doubled, showing more careful study of that part of the corporation problem. Nothing has been added to capital account, but the policy has been inaugurated of setting aside certain sums for the payment of outstanding unfunded debts. The old traffic of the company was large enough to furnish a good basis for the present better condition ; the question was one of management exclusively.

The management of American railways is better than it used to be—better as to operation and more exact as to the accounts. Nevertheless, while some railways furnish model specimens of book-keeping in their reports, others, weighed down in some cases by traditional policy in their accounting, publish statements of their finances which are misleading. For example, the practice of carrying branch-line losses as assets, wrong as the policy seems when stated in those words, nevertheless can in some cases be justified from a book-keeper's standpoint. Yet it is clear that a railway company might continue to call such deficiencies " investments in subsidiary roads," and continue to issue bonds to cover the actual cash required, until at last a poor year might not yield earnings enough to pay interest on the overloaded debt. If, at the same time, owing to the state of the money market and the spreading knowledge of the road's real condition, no one would lend it any more money, a crisis would be impending, with a certain loss to the holder of the company's bonds and perhaps an assessment on the stock. It has been assumed that the Rich Valley, though not itself earning interest, was valuable to the Great Eastern because of the interchanged traffic. In some cases these branch lines may not be worth much to the parent road, and may, indeed, have been " unloaded " on the old road by unscrupulous insiders. In judging of such cases, the ordinary stockholder must rely upon the character of the men in control. Full knowledge of such details is not usually possible to him.

But while every particular concerning a road cannot be and need not be known, it has been the purpose of this chapter to show that any one with a fair knowledge of railroad operations can find out for himself the

broad facts concerning any company, provided sufficient details are given in the annual reports, and provided he will take the trouble to examine them closely.
It is a mistake to suppose that nothing can be ascertained from the annual reports of railways ; the main
facts can be. It is often thought that the figures can
be manipulated, and so made worse than useless ; this
is true, but only to a certain degree. The items in a
railway report are interdependent in a way often un-
suspected. For example, if bonds have been issued or
bills payable contracted, some item or items on the
other side of the balance-sheet must be increased also.
The inquirer should then proceed to look into such
items of assets with a view to finding out whether such
increases are legitimate, and if so, whether they commend themselves to his judgment. Charges to capital
should be scrutinized carefully, with a glance at the
items allowed for maintaining roadbed, track, and
equipment to see whether these have been neglected.
Comparison should always be taken with a road simi-
larly situated, and more than one year's work should
be tabulated.

The lading of the trains can easily be ascertained,
while a little study will show that the number of tons
carried one mile, the rate per ton mile, the number of
train miles run, the cost of the same, and the net earnings of the company, are all related to each other.

In order that the general facts regarding a railway's
operation and financial management may be open to
investigation, public opinion should require that the
annual reports of all railways should contain statements in detail of every item of income and expense,
including statistics of trains. By following and com-
paring these statistics from year to year and studying

9

them in connection with the statements of similar rail-roads, an investor or stockholder, after the manner herein set forth, can form a fair judgment as to the main facts which affect the value of the company's bonds or stock.

CHAPTER VII

PUBLIC POLICY TOWARD CORPORATION PROFITS

IF we assume that advancement in material civilization is made possible chiefly through a cheapening of the cost of production for staple articles, and if we believe that true progress can be made only as both labor and capital receive their due rewards, we state the conditions of an industrial problem which point directly toward more effective organization. Cheaper cost, higher wages, and better profits form a union of blessings which can be realized, if realized at all, in no other way than through combinations of capital, larger in the aggregate, though divided into small ownerships, together with the best mechanical resources, a massing of employees, and an efficient oversight of the whole. Following industrial precedents, we may expect that time will be required before the greater part of our commerce in staples will be carried on by such large organizations, yet the evolution, though slow, is unmistakably in that direction.

Such organizations, so far as we can now see, can be best arranged through corporations. Just as the State may pass laws regulating the business and credit of partnerships, so it may give charters to companies and enact statutes defining their rights and responsibilities. Limited liability is the essence of the corporation idea ;

combining the possibility of gathering large amounts of capital in the forms of bonds and shares, with easy and legal ways of dividing that capital into proportions, minute yet distinct. The corporation, assured of a continued existence though its officers or shareholders may die, offers on the one side a well-understood chance to investors with risks small as compared to a partnership, and on the other an unequalled opportunity to men of first-rate administrative ability.

The relation of such trade bodies to the State and to the public may give rise to problems with which succeeding generations must deal. In the development of large corporations three parties should be benefited : the capitalist, the consumer, and the laboring man. But before the political or social economist may properly discuss the rights of the latter two as to their fair share of the larger profits which the corporate form renders attainable, there must be an acknowledgment of the fairness of good returns to the capitalist. Without a prospect of profit no capital could be obtained for investment in land, buildings, or machinery, and without this first venture of capital, few laborers could find employment. This is particularly true at the formation of the corporation, and for a reasonable number of years thereafter. With the question of the fairness of large corporation profits long continued, we are not now concerned. So far as experience goes, we may believe that commercial forces, in the majority of cases, are effective for a reduction of the profits of long-established corporations to a normal basis.

It often happens that this privilege of making money is granted by public opinion to firms and individuals, but denied to incorporated companies. It is forgotten that a corporation, particularly at the beginning, is a business enterprise as purely as a partnership. Purchasers of its bonds or shares weigh the chances of success, and usually demand concessions in some way commensurate with the supposed risks, before buying. In the case of a partnership, this practical demand for a profit in proportion to the danger of loss and the resulting uncertainty, is admitted to be equitable. It is no less so where the same business is undertaken by a company. The owner of a dwelling-house which has doubled in value collects his rent on the advanced valuation ; and no objection is made. If the house should be owned by a stock company, the doubling of the annual returns on the shares would in the minds of many be an economic offense. At the beginning the enterprise of building a costly line of elevated railway in New York City was thought to be a doubtful one. The original projector was able to secure capital enough to build an experimental piece of road, but not to demonstrate the success of the plan commercially and financially. The capitalists, who secured control and proceeded with the work of extending the lines, believed in the enterprise and backed their belief with their money ; yet many people thought failure would be the result. When afterwards success was seen to be assured, the payment of good returns in some form on the sums originally invested was believed by the capitalists who hazarded their money to be their commercial right.

Public opinion seems, indeed, to be confused between the question of the fairness of corporation dividends in ordinary cases, and the larger and more difficult question of the equity of high profits when earned by huge corporations long established and monopolistic in their nature. Yet even in these latter cases, few such companies are monopolies at the start ; they usually begin business under doubts as to their financial success, just as other companies do : their development into grasping concerns belongs rather to the second stage of the corporation problem at which the United States (speaking broadly) has hardly yet arrived.

If, then, corporations are primarily business enterprises under a new form, and if they are in consequence entitled to business profits the same as partnerships, it becomes proper to consider the tests to which the fairness of such business profits may be rightly subjected. The prevailing ideas on this subject as regards corporations are clearly inequitable, and this injustice is in great part responsible for stock-watering and other ills with which corporation finance is afflicted. Public opinion still insists that the rates of dividends paid by corporations shall be measured, as to their fairness, by the ruling rate of interest on borrowed money. It is constantly said that five or six per cent. annual returns on the share capital of a company is all that should be paid, since about that percentage is the normal yield on bonds or commercial paper or paid on notes discounted at the banks. It is overlooked that the standard thus set is the rate on money loaned on good collateral, and considered secure both as to interest and principal. The comparison may be proper as between the prevailing rate of interest and that paid by the company on its bonds ; but manifestly the returns on that part of the capital hazarded by the shareholders should not be so judged. If that rule were really carried out, if public opinion had been able to limit returns even in hazardous enterprises to a bare interest rate, the community would be the worst sufferer from the lack of facilities in transportation, in manu-

facturing, and in trading which it now enjoys. The
only result of this ill-defined but commercially erroneous opinion about the rate of dividends has been to
complicate the whole subject of corporation investment
and regulation with a series of false issues. We are
treated to long discussions and severe statutes upon
the subject of " water " in the stocks and bonds of railways and other corporations ; while the real point has
usually been the commercial justice of returns larger
than the rate of interest on borrowed money when paid
to shareholders in companies formed and managed simply as business enterprises.

The experience of all civilized countries has shown
the uselessness of all direct attempts to limit profits by
legislation. Such attempts merely compel concealment
in some way, or dull the edge of enterprise. For example, the charter of the Boston and Worcester Railroad
(now a part of the Boston and Albany), granted by
Massachusetts in 1831, has this section :

" Toll is granted as may be agreed upon by the
directors provided that if, at the expiration of ten
years, the net income from tolls and other profits shall
have amounted to more than ten per cent. per annum
upon the cost of the road, the legislature may take
measures to reduce the tolls in such a manner as to
take off the surplus."

It is agreed that the railroad in question has paid
much more than the ten per cent. yearly allowed, during the last sixty years. There is no known instance
of such a limitation of dividends being practically enforced where commercial profits justified a higher rate.
The only legislation which, under present conditions,
has much chance of practical effect, is that of which
some London (England) gas charters furnish an illus-

tration. By Act of Parliament certain of these gas companies must sell the gas at 3*s.* 9*d.* per 1000 feet. For every penny taken off this price to consumers the company is allowed to increase the dividend one fourth of one per cent. ; for every increase in the price, there must be a corresponding dividend reduction. Of course such legislation is crude, for there can be no arithmetical ratio between the prices of the goods sold and the annual dividends on the shares ; but it embodies a principle, which indeed usually works itself out in rough fashion, that there must be a division of the benefits of the corporate form between the parties concerned. It would be inequitable if a corporation should keep all the profits for its shareholders ; and equally unjust if it could so keep none of them.

It is not necessary to prove that values have increased in the United States ; figures, such as those of the census, showing such increases between 1880 and 1890, are available for those wishing to follow the subject farther. It is also a matter of common knowledge that, while certain individuals and firms have failed, others have amassed large fortunes. A number of firms have taken the corporate form and have offered their shares to the public. In no one of these cases of incorporation of old partnerships was the original amount invested in the business by the partners stated ; the public, it is held, has no right to that information. The prospectuses of the Proctor & Gamble Co., The H. B. Claflin Co., or of the larger corporations, like the American Sugar Refining Co., may be searched in vain for such information. The present status of the new company and its probable future, based upon the profits for several years past, are, however, always set forth in the prospectus, and these facts and estimates

really form the basis upon which the amount of capitalization the new company can bear is arrived at. What
percentage upon the original investment the yearly
profits to the old partners have been, is not thought to
have any bearing upon the value of the business at the
time of incorporation. The capitalization is fixed at
such an amount as will in the judgment of the promoters
allow the shares to be sold to the public at about their
par value. If the profits are legitimate, the business
stable, and the financial condition honestly set forth,
the arrangement is proper. If the enterprise had been
started originally as a corporation, it is to be feared
that the large profits annually earned would have been
considered as commercial wrongs to the community.
But whether these profits are fairly earned or not, is a
question which cannot be determined by the percentage of such profits to the original investment. Their
fairness is not alone to be judged by the rate of returns,
nor by the fact that those returns are divided among
partners or paid to shareholders by an incorporated
company.

Conceding that in fairness the value and profits of a
corporation should vary with the degree of success, and
be allowed to grow with the growth of business generally, the question arises : How should that increase
be registered ? Real estate finds purchasers at prices
which show the successive changes in values. The
property of large companies cannot be so treated. A
merchant takes an inventory on a certain day, and so
can close his books for the year with exactness. Not
so a railway, for example, whose balance-sheet must
continue on the same nominal basis of values from year
to year in order to preserve the continuity of the com
pany. Such corporations can show the daily or yearly

fluctuations in the value of their assets, and in the value of their stocks and bonds based upon those assets, only by changes in the market prices. This occasions no trouble in the case of industrial corporations whose stock is in few hands ; but in the case of companies whose shares are owned largely by persons exercising no direct control over its affairs—by investors, in short —other questions arise ; when increased profits are to be divided higher dividends must be paid or additional stock issued. Usually the stock is " watered " to make the capitalization conform in a rough way to the value of the property as determined by its probable earning capacity. During the flush times following the resumption of specie payments in 1879, the railways, particularly those west of Chicago, felt the full effects of the improved conditions and good crops. They made money rapidly. The Chicago, Rock Island, and Pacific Railway Company, for illustration, paid 9½ per cent. dividends on its then capital stock in the fiscal year ending March 31, 1879, and ten per cent. in 1880. Finding its profits still increasing, the company, in June, 1880, doubled its capital stock, giving to the holders two shares for one. The prognostications of its officers were for the moment justified, for the company on its doubled shares paid 6½ per cent. in dividends in 1881, and seven per cent. in 1882.

Stock-watering in this, its innocent form, is not an attempt to cover up extortion, so much as to solve a commercial question. It is not a cause of an increase in profits, but rather an effect of such increase, whose fairness toward customers should be judged in other ways and by other means. The prejudice in the public mind against the distribution of dividends by corporations at a percentage higher than the usual

interest upon loans, makes the public itself in a measure responsible for such shares of unpaid stocks as are
issued to conceal the fact that the earnings are larger
than the usual borrowing rate.

The remedy for stock-watering, therefore, even in its
innocent form, is not additional law but a change in
public opinion, which shall allow the payment of ten,
twelve, or fifteen per cent., if legitimately earned, to
the shareholders of corporations organized for business
purposes. It would certainly be a gain in honesty if
the capital of a company could openly be stated at a
sum no larger than the amount actually invested.
This would be the result much oftener than now if such
returns as are above suggested could, without protest
—because of that fact,—be paid if earned. But this is
not all. The community by its feeling against high
corporation dividends deprives itself of a certain natural
protection against unfair earnings; because if such
were openly paid competition would be oftener at-
tracted. The tendency of an open return would be
toward a lower return. In the case of the Chicago,
Rock Island, and Pacific Company just mentioned, the
extreme profitableness of traffic-carrying in the years
following 1880 was found not to be lasting. After paying seven per cent. in dividends upon the doubled stock
yearly, from 1882 to 1887, the company distributed but
four per cent. in the years from 1889 to 1893, thus
bringing the real returns to about the same rate as
ruled before the watering. Had the original capital
not been doubled this latter return would not seem so
small. What the community has lost in freights and
facilities, through the efforts of the managers to pay
dividends on doubled capital at a rate which should
nominally be as high as the usual interest on borrowed
money, can only be a matter of conjecture.

The tendency of corporation managers, under the pressure of public protest against high dividends, to water the capital has been much accelerated by the financial law that stock-watering actually increases market values. If a company is paying ten per cent. annually in dividends, its shares will be quoted, let us say, at 175. If now the company doubles the number of its shares and continues to pay five per cent., its new stock will be quoted at about par. The original holder, while receiving the same aggregate dividends as before, finds his principal increased in value. The same law holds good when shares are below par. If a company's stock is quoted at sixty, and a stock dividend of fifty per cent. be declared, the quotations will not fall to forty as they ought. This fact, probably explainable on the previously mentioned theory that share values are in part based on the interest rate, has always been a strong incentive to stock-watering.

Another objection to stock-watering is that while it provides a method by which capitalization and profits may correspondingly increase, it affords no means of registering a decline in those profits, for shares once issued cannot readily be found and called in. In speculative America fluctuations in business profits are to be expected, and one of the embarrassing things in Wall Street is the presence there of shares having little or no intrinsic value but which may be used by unscrupulous and sometimes almost penniless adventurers to obtain possession of a railway or other company. The temptation in such cases is great for the men thus placed in control to recoup themselves in some way for the cost of purchasing that control. Low-priced stocks cannot, of course, be avoided, but their number might be largely decreased if we could remove from the exchanges those shares which represent "water" principally, and which have fallen below the expectations of optimistic stock-waterers. The well-known early history of the Erie Railway furnishes a good illustration. Yet here, as before, we must first remove the cause of the trouble ; namely, the public feeling against good corporation profits based upon the original investment. The argument of the stock-waterer always is, that in no other way can he secure profits commensurate with his risks, even if fairly earned ; and it is an argument which has its force.

While the amount of capitalization has little effect upon the rates charged by the railways—for it is in reference to railways that the question has been most discussed—the indirect results of excessive capitalization are evil. If a company's capital stock has been doubled and the shares now receive (let us say) five per cent., these shares are sold to innocent holders on the basis of a five per cent. return. If, for any reason, the dividend should be reduced to four per cent. there are immediate protests from the then shareholders, for the reason that the apparent returns are below the nominal rates of interest. But if, on the other hand, the company had been allowed to continue payments of ten per cent. upon the original number of shares, that percentage of payment for good commercial reasons could be reduced to eight per cent. without so much complaint —the reduction in the actual earnings of the company being the same in both cases. It is because of this that, when a decline in profit comes, stock-watering has a direct effect. The managers knowing that a reduction in the dividend rate from four to five per cent. will be very unpopular, strive in every way legitimately and illegitimately to continue the old payments. They will withdraw trains, will discharge employees, will buy less supplies, and in every way will endeavor to increase their net earnings up to the former amount, with the result that the public are deprived of facilities to which they are entitled and which they might otherwise obtain ; while at the same time the industrial depression is aggravated by the larger number of men thrown out of work directly through the action of the company in their discharge and indirectly in the refusal to purchase the usual amount of material and supplies. Here, again, the condemnation goes farther than complaints against the existing management and touches the source of the trouble, viz., the attempts of the company, perhaps years before, to placate public opinion while at the same time paying the high dividends to which its shareholders considered themselves entitled. There is reason for thinking that the former lack of train service on the New York City Elevated and the deficiency in other facilities (such as the proper lighting of the cars), of which loud and frequent complaints were made, can be traced back to the time when the owners, finding their projected profits more than five or six per cent. on the original cost, issued the watered stock of the Manhattan Company to correspond with the expected increase in dividends. Had public opinion allowed the payment of ten or twelve or fifteen per cent. on the original capitalization, it is possible that better service would have afterwards been given, even though the dividends had then been reduced to eight per cent. Public opinion against high corporation returns is thus responsible indirectly for the later public complaints of overcrowding and other ills.

What has been considered may be called the inno-

cent form of stock-watering. But all stock-watering is
not innocent. An unreal prosperity may be brought
about through an illegitimate curtailing of expenses
and in other ways, so that an extra issue of stock may
falsely be made to seem justifiable on grounds of large
but fair profits. Or honest prosperity may come up
quickly, to fall away as quickly. In either case, whether
through fraud or error, the increase of capital stock
may be commercially unwarranted and a source of loss
to innocent investors. Again, parties in control of a
railroad or other large corporation owning comparatively few shares, may decide suddenly to distribute
new shares free ; and, by taking advantage of their ex-
clusive information, may, if unrestrained, make large
sums of money for themselves. Or, further, a company's directors, to perpetuate their control, may issue
new shares to themselves at merely the cost and trouble
of buying old shares on a margin. This may result in
giving over to men not equitably the real owners, the
management of an important property. Such control
is not likely to be exercised for the public good, but
rather for speculative purposes. Such stock-watering
as this is an abuse of the principles of good corporation
finance, against which it is the right of the State to
protect itself by all legitimate means. Yet, until high
returns are freely allowed, the distinction between the
right and the wrong of the practice is one always to be
borne in mind. The laws of New York State regarding railways try to meet this difficulty. Its statutes
provide that no increase of capital stock shall be valid
unless approved by a two-thirds vote of the shareholders at a meeting called for that purpose after
twenty days' notice to each stockholder, and unless
also approved by the Board of Railroad Commissioners.

A further amendment, passed in 1890, adds that no
stock shall be issued except for money, labor, or property. In passing upon applications for increase, the
Board since 1883 has wisely interpreted the statute as
not condemning such issues where cause is shown.
The Board consents to an increase when the new stock
is to be sold and the proceeds spent upon the property ;
but if the stock is to be distributed free, then the total
capitalization (bonds and stock) must not exceed the
cost of the property. It is the custom to include in the
term cost, all improvements paid out for revenue.
Practically, therefore, when such an unpaid issue seems
expedient for sound commercial reasons, but little
stands in the way of the Board's approval ; for expenditures on the property above cost of mere maintenance from year to year can usually be shown by all
prosperous roads ; yet it would be better to increase
dividends than to increase the capitalization. On the
other hand, the New York statutes have apparently
stopped, or at least rendered very difficult, the fraudulent cases of stock issue just referred to. The necessary vote of so large a proportion of stockholders after
a three-weeks notice of the reason for calling them
together, renders the action of a minority-holding Board
of Directors practically impossible should such a board
attempt to give money or control to themselves by a
sudden issue. The real owners must first approve of
the plan. Then the public stockholders' meeting and
the public argument before, and investigation by, the
Board of Railroad Commissioners take·so much time
that all concerned have an opportunity in which to
arrange their holdings for the change. There is, of
course, the further objection to any issue of share
capital without full payment, however justified by

trade circumstances, that it really gives to a holder at
once and at a particular time that increase in value
which may have been accruing for years. But by such
laws as these of New York, the State, until public
opinion as to corporation profits changes, has gone as
far as it rightfully can to protect all interests. No
statute can give exact justice, to every complainant.
To stop all free issues of stock, even the innocent, would,
in the present state of opinion upon the unfairness of
high corporate dividends, put a check upon corporate
enterprise which would work injury to the public as a
whole. The State selfishly wishes its capitalists to
realize enough returns from incorporated capital so
that as many railroads as are needed may be built,
the public thus getting facilities in transportation not
otherwise attainable. The State of Massachusetts in
1894 enacted amendments to its railroad laws, which
forbid the free issue of stock under any circumstances ;
issues of shares are lawful only after approval by the
Board of Railroad Commissioners and for the purposes
certified to, and must be sold to shareholders at auction
at not less than par, or at the market value if more
than par. Such absolute prohibition of stock-watering
is economically justifiable only where no limit is put
upon corporation dividends either in public opinion or
indirectly through legislation intended arbitrarily to
reduce charges.

10

CHAPTER VIII

CORPORATION REORGANIZATIONS AND RECEIVER-SHIPS

ALTHOUGH as has already been stated, the corporation form is best adapted for those businesses which meet a public demand, whose volume of trading or traffic or manufacture is apparently steady, and whose profits under good management may be expected to be reasonably uniform, and although under such conditions insolvency should be rare, yet incorporated companies at times become bankrupt—that is, are unable to pay their floating or funded debts. If such corporate insolvencies in any line of business constitute a larger percentage than is shown by the general average throughout the United States, a percentage larger either in the proportion of bankrupts to the whole or in the proportion of assets to liabilities, then it is important for the welfare both of investors and of the public that careful investigation should be made to ascertain the causes of such undue percentages. Perhaps the reasons for such large proportion of bankrupts may lie in the fact that the earnings of the company from some cause have been reduced so fast that the expenses could not correspondingly be cut down ; or it may be that the capitalization of the company was in the first place arranged on a false basis; or perhaps the failure may have come from a combination of these causes. Sometimes, also, widespread commercial disasters, such as the failures of crops over a large section of the country, may account for the temporary embarrassment ; although even in such a case the possibility, in a concern whose finances have been conservatively managed, ought long ago to have been taken into account.

But from whatever cause arising or whatever the percentage may be of those companies which have failed to have achieved success, the fact of the inability of any company to pay its debts brings up at once a large number of financial problems of extreme difficulty and delicacy. The affairs of the simple trading company, when forced to succumb, may prove comparatively easy of adjustment ; but not so with large companies. Our great railway systems, for example, have grown to their present size by degrees through the construction or absorption into the system of lines or branches once independent, or which may yet be nominally considered so. The credit of such a huge railway system is also a matter of growth; but a good credit once attained does not yield easily to the first rumor of disaster. The managers, properly careful for the interest of the shareholders, put the best face upon the declining revenues in the hope that the deficit may be but temporary—and indeed by helping to tide over a period of embarrassment through the means of old established credit, the managers of such a system have in many instances really saved the property for the shareholders. In other cases, however, where the evil was too deep seated to be removed or where the embarrassment continued so long that it could be no longer ignored, the confession of insolvency has found the affairs of the company in a most unfortunate shape.

The receivers, upon appointment, have been ordered by the court to pay off those back debts which properly should have been discharged at the time of their incurring from current revenues, but which were allowed to accumulate in order to enable the managers to maintain the appearance of solvency. As these claims are made a first lien upon the property either with or without the issue of receivers' certificates, usually the property must remain in receivers' hands at least as long as it may be necessary to accumulate from the revenues sums sufficient to provide for these prior claims. If, after a time, it is found that the payment of these claims from revenues is impossible, or where receivers' certificates have been issued for this very purpose and are now outstanding, then these sums must be taken into account by the reorganizers of the company as so much which must be raised by the owners of the property before it can be turned over to them.

In addition to the sums of money thus directly required, it is almost always found that other cash amounts are also necessary. Since a railway system does not plunge at once into insolvency, it usually finds itself tending in that direction for a longer or shorter time previous to the final confession, and it commonly happens during these months or years when the stress of the circumstances began to bear hard upon them, that the managers have omitted to do many things which the business of the company really required. In the case of railways the roadbed may have been long neglected without absolutely going below the standard of safety. Repairs to wooden bridges or trestles have been delayed and renewals of rails and ties have been put off, so that the real requirements of the property are not revealed until a receivership makes concealment no longer advisable. When that receivership comes and before reorganization plans can be drawn up, the amount of money necessary to be spent in order to make good all depreciation and to render the plant capable of the most economic working must be definitely known. This is the time, too, for an outlook into the future when the possible changes in transportation rates or in the services demanded should be met by some arrangement for granting to the reorganized company certain sums of money year by year for this future use. Altogether the cash requirements for the present and for the future constitute sums which must be raised in reorganization either by assessments upon the shares and bonds or—what amounts to the same thing — by some arrangement which will allow of a prior mortgage upon the property sufficient to accomplish these results. Usually, also, it is necessary that the accounts of the defaulting company should be gone over carefully in order that the real earnings of the property, unadulterated through bookkeeping assets or suspense accounts or padding of any kind, should be ascertained.

With these figures before them and with the outlook for business in general and in the section of the country immediately concerned in particular, the banking firm or committee are able to determine within reasonable limits what the earning power of the company after reorganization will be. Here, then, are the elements of the problem at the beginning. A certain amount of cash must be raised to pay off debts and to make good the deficiencies in the depreciation account ; allowance must be made for the cash requirements of the future ; and finally all the fixed charges of the reorganized company must be brought so far below the assumed earnings as to give to the new bonded capital a good standing and credit at once upon all the exchanges.

It having been determined to what extent the present bond- and shareholders must suffer loss in order to bring the capital of the new company within the earning limits at the time of reorganization, the next problem is the division of this loss among the old security holders. This is a task demanding the widest knowledge combined with the best financial judgment. Under our assumption the railway system, now insolvent, is composed of many different parts, each having upon it bonds varying in value, in interest charges, and in length of time to maturity, whose liens upon the various properties may also be so interlaced as to make their disentanglement a very difficult thing indeed. Very likely there are prior lien mortgages upon the older parts of the road on which the interest charges have unquestionably been earned. Where such is clearly the case, such bonds should not be asked to surrender any part of their principal or interest. A fundamental axiom in corporation financiering is that bonds which are unquestionably good should unquestionably be paid. Nothing tends to throw discredit upon corporation securities so much as a lack of discrimination in cases of insolvency between bonds which are good and those which are not.

Perhaps there is also a first mortgage upon the entire system whose interest has been earned ; if so, the loss should fall upon the junior securities ; or perhaps one of the difficulties of reorganization begins at this point. It may be that the main line has earned the interest on these first-mortgage bonds, to judge from the statements prepared in the auditor's office ; but it is important to inquire whence comes the traffic whose

carriage has yielded this profit?   There may be branch
lines which give to the system so much of its volume
of business that without them interest on the first-mortgage bonds would not have been earned ; it may be
that valuable terminals in the large cities are occupied
by the company subject to mortgages of their own : or,
again, perhaps contracts of various kinds have been
entered into with connecting roads which on their face
are unprofitable, and yet if those contracts were an-
nulled the resulting indirect loss to the company might
seriously imperil the interest on the first mortgage
which we are considering.   Manifestly, in the face of
such complications, it will not do to say that interest on
these first-mortgage bonds has been earned and should
be paid, while at the same time no allowance is made
for interest upon the terminal bonds or branch-line
obligations or contracts with connecting lines.   If it is a
question of division of the losses between them, the
exact proportion which each should suffer can only be
determined after a careful search into the whole matter and after a full investigation into the claims of each
one of these from a transportation point of view.

It is, in a majority of cases, useless for the holders
of bonds having a lien upon a specific piece of road to
think of foreclosing their mortgage and taking the
property covered by it out of the system to make it
independent.   An exception, of course, must be made
in the cases of property such as a terminal in a large
city, which may be essential to the business of the defaulting company and yet which may be so situated as
to be easily turned over to and used by some other
company.   In such cases, of course, there is no alternative but to keep such terminals in the system by
paying interest upon the bonds ; usually the courts are

quick to recognize the exigencies of the situation and
to authorize the receivers to pay such interest even at
the expense of the remaining parts of the trust estate.
Usually, however, a piece of property, even though
covered by a separate mortgage, finds its chief value as
a component part of the system as a whole. The
reason for the amalgamation of separate railways into
one system is that the business as a whole may be
administered to the best advantage of all. Under
these conditions the individuality of any one part of
the system is in time lost and cannot be easily regained
even under a separate ownership through foreclosure
of that particular mortgage. There is something,
therefore, beyond mere words in the disinclination so
often stated by the courts to allow any " disintegration
of the system," and there is likewise good reason for
the further order that at any sale for the purposes of reorganization the whole shall be offered as one parcel.
This is the true policy, not only from the point of view
of the investor which we have just been considering,
but also from that of the public whose facilities for
quick and cheap transportation would be seriously inter-
fered with, were an old system allowed to be broken
into its separate parts by reason of differences of opinion between the bondholders as to the values of their
respective mortgages. The same reasoning with modi-
fications suited to the circumstances applies to corporations other than railways which have been conducting
large business operations.

Stockholders to whom belong all the profits of the
enterprise should under ordinary circumstances be willing to bear the losses. It is upon this principle that
the cash requirements of an insolvent company, which
have just been referred to, are usually made up by an

assessment upon the shares. But this principle is itself limited by expediency. If, under the influence of
impending trouble and actual insolvency, the quotations for the shares on the exchanges have fallen to
very low figures, a large assessment levied upon each
share might indeed, if carried out, result in the wiping
out of such stock under a reorganization, but would not
bring into the treasury of the new company any cash ;
the old shareholders would prefer to lose their holdings
rather than to pay the assessment demanded, unless
they were convinced that the prices of the new shares
upon the exchanges after reorganization would at least
be higher than the amount of the assessment. If the
shares alone are asked to furnish the money for the
cash requirements and at the same time to stand the
brunt of the reorganization generally, the new stock
to be given in exchange for the assessment might be
of little value. From the nature of the case the
equities of a reorganization cannot be proved like a
mathematical problem, but are matters of individual
judgment ; hence able lawyers employed by aggrieved
shareholders are often able to bring forward facts and
arguments to such an extent as to make doubtful or
delay the carrying out of any plan of reorganization to
which their clients are unanimously opposed. More
than that, the mortgages, under whose terms the bondholders must act in foreclosing, often contain sections
whose exact meaning perhaps is doubtful, or whose
provisions cannot be quickly carried out, offering
chances for long legal delays. It is sometimes possible
for the shareholders to oppose the foreclosure of a
mortgage so skilfully as to make the carrying out a
matter of years. For all these reasons it is customary
in drawing up plans of reorganization to consult the

so-called " rights " of the stockholder to as great a
degree as is consistent with justice to all concerned.

The practical effect of this small deference to the
shareholder is to put a part of the losses under reorganization upon the junior securities ; that is, upon those
mortgages which of course come ahead of the stock,
but whose lien upon the property is subsequent to the
older bonds. Perhaps the cash requirements already
spoken of may be arranged for by an assessment of
several dollars upon each share of stock and also upon
the junior bonds. Sometimes when the future looks
hopeful, the holders of the senior bonds may be asked
to forego their interest for a while or to refund their
coupons into a separate loan for which they may receive other securities under the plan.

In the history of American railway reorganizations,
it has been a common thing to find certain bonds or
shares given to the old holders, to represent the cash
assessments which they were asked to pay, or the
losses in principal or interest to which they were
asked to submit. Such a course is justified by business
conditions in the United States. In America values
are largely determined by reference to the future.
Quotations of the corporation stocks or bonds upon
the exchanges are governed by two considerations—the
present earnings and the expectation for the future.
Such a method of estimating values is to be expected
in a large country not yet fully developed, whose agricultural and mineral possibilities are great, and which
on the average is increasing in wealth and in the
volume of business year by year. The very pace by
which industry usually advances leaves the way open
for temporary depreciations, and these for a time may
curtail business to such an extent as to leave a railway

or other corporation unable to meet its obligations. If, under these circumstances reorganization becomes necessary, it is not forgotten that the future may have in store for the company greater earnings than are now annually being obtained. Hence it is in accordance with business facts that the holders of bonds or shares which, under the stress of present necessity, must sacrifice something, should ask that some evidence of their former claims against the company be granted them. They ask for this evidence so that if the company in future years should earn as much as in times of former prosperity or indeed anything at all beyond the present standard, these old postponed claims may then become alive again and be worth something to their holders. Nearly all railway reorganizations recognize the justice of this position, and the plans are arranged accordingly.

Another reason why the method of giving some evidences of indebtedness in exchange for assessments or bond losses is popular, lies in the fact that investment sentiment seems better satisfied where paper of some kind is given to bondholders in return for their sacrifices, than where such sacrifices are demanded without it. This is true even in cases where the intrinsic values of the two pieces of paper are no larger than that of one alone would be. But even where intrinsically the same, it is a common experience that the quotations for the two are larger than would be that for one alone. The great majority of mankind are optimists and deal with corporations' shares and securities optimistically. The natural hopes of investors, therefore, serve to give to an income bond or a share of stock dependent upon future earnings, a quotable value which through sentiment may be considerably higher than that justified by the present position of the company.

For these reasons it may be possible in an easily arranged plan of reorganization to give to the holder of a discredited bond a new bond for a part of his claims, and in addition an income bond or shares of preferred stock, in such proportion that by selling both new issues the old bondholder may be able to get back his entire investment and really lose nothing. Such a procedure, however, is oftentimes possible only when the capitalization of the new company is largely increased. If regard is had to the present time only and to the demands of the present holders of the bonds of the defaulting company, such a reorganization will be considered a success; and it is not to be denied that the wish to satisfy present demands is legitimate so far as it may be proper. But if we regard the day of reckoning, such a reorganization may not be defensible. The new capitalization may indeed be made to mature long years hence, but when that maturity arrives and the increased principal must be met, the wrongfulness of a plan which increases the capitalization, even though without an increase of obligatory charges at the moment, becomes apparent. And if, meanwhile other disasters should overtake the corporation, the old injudicious arrangement of increased capitalization will make it all the more difficult to secure to the company such new money or such concessions as it may need.

When the holders of discredited bonds are asked to surrender a part of their principal and to accept a smaller rate of interest, an income bond to represent the losses may be offered to them. To satisfy the conditions of the problem, this bond must be of such a' character as to be quoted in the Street at such a figure as will reimburse the old holders for their sacrifices; at the same time, of course, the object of the reorganization must be kept in view—that is, to reduce the fixed charges. To satisfy both these conditions, the income bond must be made contingent upon earnings on the one hand, and on the other must have also such obligatory features as will commend it to investors. Although these two features are contradictory, such a bond has, in a number of cases, been arranged for in American reorganizations. Experience has shown what, indeed, might have been expected, that such a form of corporation capital works out no better in practice than in theory. On the one side, the holders of such income or preference bonds are continually claiming that certain profits earned by the railway company should be paid over to them. On the other hand, the principal being an obligation, these income or preference bonds often stand in the way of proper management of the finances of the company. As every growing system has increasing needs, the managers find easy opportunities where the expenditure of a few thousands of dollars would bring a large return in the way of increased traffic or profit ; yet they are debarred from borrowing money because the income mortgages deny them that privilege. The result of this curious position is that the company does not progress as it ought, the acuteness of the managers being meanwhile exercised to devise means whereby the too stringent terms of the income mortgage may be made practically of no effect. For illustration, a company may need larger terminals, and these terminals may be the means of increasing the profits which should go toward paying something upon the income bonds. Being, however, unable in its own name to borrow the money to pay for these terminals (because the new mortgage cannot be put ahead of the income bonds), the company may arrange to have them held in another name, meanwhile entering into a contract with the terminal company to pay over to the latter certain sums for the use of the supposed terminals. Such a terminal charge per passenger and per ton is agreed upon as will be enough to meet the interest on the new terminal bonds ; such terminal charges being meanwhile added to the working expenses of the system. In this way practically the interest on the terminal bonds is paid for by the parent company, although the terms of the income or preferred mortgage would forbid such a thing if attempted directly. All these considerations being taken into account, the quotations for these income bonds often rule so low upon the stock exchanges as to make a large issue necessary if the original losses of the bondholders under reorganization are to be thus made up. As a consequence, the capitalization of the new company is much larger than that of the old.

Preferred stocks given in exchange for the sacrifices of the old bondholders are much better than income bonds from the point of view of good corporation financiering. Preferred shares may thus properly represent deferred claims. There is no peremptory obligation resting upon the company to pay an annual dividend upon these shares, particularly if they are made noncumulative. To make dividends on preferred shares cumulative is not good policy except in extreme cases, because it lays the shares open in modified degree to the reasoning which has just been applied to the income bonds. Preferred shares, too, have voting power, and their holders, even though small in number, are thus put in the way of defending their own interests in the Board of Directors or before it. Moreover, while an excessive capitalization represented by

shares is an evil and gives rise to some objectionable conditions in our corporation finance, yet it is by no means
so dangerous as excessive capital represented by bonds.
Altogether, therefore, preferred shares represent deferred claims under reorganization much better than
can income or preference bonds, and in all cases of
reorganization should be issued for such purposes
where the laws of the state will allow of such issue.
The issue of preferred shares in exchange for assessments paid by the common-stock holders is often made
expedient by the sentimental wish of the assessed
shareholder to have some special piece of paper to
represent his payments.

Legally the owner of a single bond is entitled to all
the rights and advantages which the terms of the mortgage may give. It is becoming more common, however,
to limit the rights of a small minority by modifying
somewhat the extreme language of the mortgage. Railway mortgages now usually provide that the trustees
shall take legal proceedings, shall declare the principal
due and shall proceed to foreclose, only when a certain
percentage of the bondholders request it so to act. Custom yet gives to one half of the bonds outstanding, or
sometimes to a smaller percentage, the right to demand
the satisfaction of their mortgage through the trustee.
But the legal right of foreclosure is one thing and the
commercial expediency is often quite another. A system with a number of different classes of bonds upon it
being in difficulties, the holders of some of the junior
issues may be unwilling to agree to any plan of reorganization whatever, or may find fault with the proportion of new securities to be given them under the
advertised plan. In either case one half or more of the
bondholders have the power to compel the trustees to

begin foreclosure proceedings.   If these proceedings
are carried through, these same bondholders must be
prepared to bid in the property in order to secure their
debt.   This, in turn, involves " financing " the new
company.   They must often be prepared to furnish
money enough at the sale to pay all the floating and
current indebtedness, and if they would make a success
of their new company, they must also be ready to
furnish the capital which under our assumed conditions the system needs in order to be put in good
condition and ready for economical working.   These
two requirements may call for so much money that the
bondholders may well hesitate before they enter upon
such an undertaking.   Holders of corporation securities are scattered throughout the country, and perhaps
many of the bonds are held in Europe.   A scattered
majority stands rather helpless before such a problem ;
the trustee will not act unless expenses are guaranteed
to it, while no banking house will undertake the formation of a new company unless it sees clearly that the
conditions favor success, and unless, too, it has the
support of a majority of the mortgage issues.   It is
customary now for committees to be formed to protect
the interests of the various securities involved in the
insolvency.   If such committee succeed in getting the
greater part of the securities deposited with it, it becomes a factor in the reorganization ; yet even when
this is the case, such committee may not be willing to
furnish the large sums necessary to finance the new
company in a manner favorable to the particular bonds
held by them.

It will thus be seen that it is better for the bondholders of a bankrupt railway system to accept a plan
of reorganization, if found equitable, rather than to

attempt to buy in the property for themselves. If the proposed plan of rehabilitation is believed by a majority of all bondholders to be unfair, it will usually fall to the ground through lack of support ; that is, a plan, to be carried out successfully, must have the active assistance of a majority of the bondholders given to it through a deposit of bonds of those holders who assent to the plan. No matter how strong the language of the mortgage, the bonds issued under it are worth only what the commercial conditions of the company allow ; hence it is better for the holders of defaulted bonds to accept a plan when found upon examination to be equitable, than to insist upon their legal rights ; for their bonds are worth only what their proportion of the total value of the company's property comes to ; they could not get any more than that proportion even though they insisted upon the full terms of the mortgage. Corporation reorganizations resolve themselves into commercial problems rather than legal.

As business conditions change rapidly in a developing country, it frequently happens that a company when insolvent and about to be reorganized wishes to get rid of certain branches, guaranties, leases, or other contracts which in the course of time may have proven themselves very unprofitable. So long as the corporation is solvent, the question of the justice of living up to its contracts does not arise. When, however, it confesses that it is unable to pay its debts, then its financial rehabilitation becomes a question of commercial value, and in this light it is deemed proper for a reorganization committee to plan for a cutting off of those branches, leases, or other contracts which are recognized as burdensome upon the company. Sometimes a company is rehabilitated without a sale of its property at foreclosure.   In such happy cases it has been found possible to make such an arrangement among all the bond- and stockholders as enables the old company to rearrange its mortgages and shares and go on with its business under the existing charter.   In cases, however, where unprofitable branch lines have had to be supported or onerous contracts carried out, the determination to relieve the company from these burdens proves a stumbling-block to the easy form of rehabilitation just referred to ; for whenever a company is rehabilitated by a change in its financial arrangements and proceeds with its business under its old charter, all the contracts, guaranties, and leases which it may once have entered into are kept alive and become claims against the company.   The only method of getting rid of such burdensome guaranties or leases is through the foreclosure of some one of the mortgages and a sale of the property and franchises to another company.   If there is a charter in existence whose privileges are such as to meet the conditions of the insolvent company, then the property may be sold and conveyed to a company organized under it.   If this is not possible, then a new charter must be obtained in the state or states concerned.

It is at this point that new difficulties arise.   In many cases the charters under which the insolvent systems are now operating were granted many years ago and contain privileges which could not now be obtained from any legislature or from congress.   It may be that the state which originally gave the franchise has, since granting that charter, enacted new laws which forbid perhaps the very things that the old charter permits.   Under these circumstances the foreclosure of one of the mortgages on the system and the sale of the property to a company formed under a new charter might involve the surrender of so much of the old commercial rights as would render the success of the enterprise doubtful. Here, again, it may be expedient for the holders of a senior or a junior mortgage to make some concessions which will allow of a restoration of the plant into the hands of the original company, rather than to insist upon the carrying out of the provisions of the mortgage, which, though legally clear, are impossible of fulfilment except at the expense of the holders of the bonds themselves. When systems having old and valuable state or federal charters have also burdensome leases or contracts, the adjustment becomes one of great difficulty. If the present charter be retained, the onerous contract is still in force even though temporarily disowned by the receivers ; if it is sought to throw off these contracts by a sale to a company newly organized under present laws, an equally large or even larger loss may be entailed. If neither party will yield something under these conditions, the property may stay in the hands of receivers much longer than would be otherwise necessary, and longer too than the courts prefer to keep the control in their possession. If at last neither will yield, it becomes a choice of evils. It may be that during the period of embarrassment the general business of the company has suffered to such an extent that the senior bonds are affected. It then becomes a question whether these senior bonds will foreclose their mortgage and let the property go for what it will bring ; in such cases the breaking up of large and important systems is a thing to be lamented in the interest of the public no less than that of the creditors themselves.

Before insolvent companies undergo reorganization there is usually a period of receivership. The practice of operating insolvent railways through court officers appointed for the purpose is not yet definitely settled either as to the methods of working or as to the legal doctrines involved, the whole matter being yet in a state of evolution.   It is the boast of our law that it changes to meet the changing demands of commerce as business becomes more complex and the rules governing it necessarily more involved ; so as regards railway receiverships our present situation is the result of a compromise between the terms of railway mortgages and the commercial conditions under which railway operations are carried on.

The original idea of appointing a receiver to take charge of the property of a firm or individual was that the business might be wound up with as little delay as possible and the assets sold and distributed to the creditors in some equitable proportion.   As corporations became more common, taking the place of firms and individuals, the same idea was applied to them when insolvent.   They were placed in the hands of receivers in order that their affairs might be closed up with the least possible delay by dividing the assets among the creditors in the proportion to which it was shown they were entitled.   It was inevitable that the question of the proper method of treating insolvency among railway companies should arise.   From small beginnings the number of miles of railway in the United States increased rapidly until now, judged by the magnitude of the property invested and the amount of business done, the railways form perhaps our largest industry, certainly one of the most complex.   Through one cause or another it was inevitable that bankruptcy should increase among these rail carriers as their mileage increased ; and in such cases also it was natural, as in the cases of firms or small corporations, that receivers should be appointed pending a settlement of the insolvent debtor's affairs. But here a new question arose. A trading firm or corporation unable to pay its debts could be wound up and its assets distributed to its creditors without loss to the community. Other traders could take their places and business would go on as before ; but it was otherwise with the railways. It was quickly seen that great states and sections of states depended upon the continued operation of these railways for the transaction of their everyday business, for supplies of clothing and manufactured goods, and even for meat and bread. Whatever the outcome, the trains must be kept running. Since, in the course of time, local railways have grown into systems, it was found that the interests involved in these systems were so enormous that their combined assets could not be easily sold as one parcel to any one person or company, or sold separately without breaking up the systems. Hence, until the serious questions of reorganization or sale were settled, the receivers of these systems must continue to run the trains in the interest of the public. As these necessary adjustments were often found very complicated, requiring a long time for negotiations and final agreement, the receivers appointed by the courts were placed for the time being in the position of railway managers. They were confronted with technical problems of much practical importance. They were required to become familiar with disputed questions concerning reasonable rates and their ramifications. The conflicting claims of cities and towns as to charges which should be relatively fair to each were pressed upon their attention. In short, it was required that receivers should be able to formulate for the operation of the properties in their charge a policy which should be equitable to the capitalists whose money was invested in the road, to all the sections served by the railway, and to the general travelling and shipping public. Needless to say, the success of such a task required men of administrative ability, with the further result that the courts through their appointed officers were obliged to decide upon the details of administration.

It was the practice at first for receivers to be asked for solely by certain creditors of the company in order that their property might be held together and protected against the seizure of certain parts of the system by other creditors which might destroy the value of the property as a whole. Usually the corporation appeared before the court in opposition to the motion, so that, if receivers were appointed at all, the court acted upon information brought to its knowledge after a severe legal struggle. The idea that the corporation itself could ask for an appointment of a receiver for its own property originated with the late Jay Gould, whose contention in the Wabash cases in this respect was afterwards affirmed by the Supreme Court of the United States, which held that a company could itself ask for the protection of the court if such was for the best interest of all concerned. Under this doctrine few of our large railway systems are now placed in any but " friendly " hands. In such cases the matter is all planned out beforehand and the men chosen. Any creditor of the company, friendly to the administration, may allege that the corporation owes him money that it cannot pay, and as every going concern has plenty of creditors in the ordinary course of business, such a convenient creditor is usually not hard to find. To this complaint, usually prepared in secret, some one of the company's officers arranges a reply confessing the truth of the charge. All parties concerned, each with the respective documents, and without notice to the other creditors or to the public, apply to the judge, perhaps at night, who forthwith grants the application and appoints the receivers already arranged for. That this procedure opens the door to the possibility of great abuse of corporate interests needs no argument. That on the whole the plan has worked fairly well is owing to the high character of our judiciary and also of the officers in charge of our great corporations. Yet it is not reassuring to holders of stocks, bonds, or floating debt to know that a conspiracy between any small creditor and any one of the principal officers of a corporation may throw the control of the whole property of the company into the hands of the court. Unquestionably, the appointment of former officers of the company as receivers leads to the charge at times that those who had wrecked the company are still left in power. Moreover, the door is open to abuses, such as the difficulty easily thrown in the way of a thorough investigation into the company's condition, which it may be the wish of the old managers to thwart, but which may be necessary before an equitable plan of reorganization can be evolved. Yet the affairs of our large corporations have become so complicated that only those long familiar with them are capable of administering them without losses both to owners of the road and to shippers. This business fact has so far controlled the action of the courts in the appointing of old officers of the insolvent corporation as receivers, though usually other men not previously connected with the company, but representing important interests as well as the sections through which the road runs, are chosen to serve with them. Laws have been introduced in various states to check the abuses to which the methods of receiverships have given rise, but while these statutes have done good as to certain matters of detail, the commercial facts of which we have spoken have been strong enough thus far to prevent any material modification of the policy.

The immediate cause of a railway receivership is usually the floating debt. Strictly speaking, the expression " floating debt " means the money borrowed by a company on collateral and made payable on demand or within a short time. The term, however, is sometimes used to cover other debts of the corporation, such as for supplies which have been bought but not paid for. A railway which is fairly prosperous can arrange to pay its bond interest in a period of depression without showing signs of distress. Every large business concern, such as a manufactory, must arrange for a depreciation of plant and machinery before setting aside earnings applicable to interest or dividends. The reason for this is that, were a contrary course to be pursued, the stock- or bondholders would very shortly find themselves in possession of a worthless property. In factories the expected losses from depreciation are usually arranged for by setting aside a certain sum of money from the earnings yearly, but the practice of railways is different. It is the custom with them to renew or replace roadbed, track, and equipment from year to year as fast as these deteroriate or become worn out, charging the cost directly to working expenses. By these means the whole plant is kept up to its standard at the expense of the earnings, the effect being the same as though specific sums had been set aside from income each year. This method of arranging for depreciation allows the railways to vary the amount of replacement from year to year according as the seasons are prosperous or the reverse. In a good year more may be spent upon the roadbed and the track and for the purchase of new equipment to replace the old at the cost of working expenses, than perhaps was proportionately required. Then, in poor years, not so much of this sort of work may be done, allowing a larger proportion of gross income to be payable to bond- and stockholders. This saving in the working expenses by a stoppage of repairs to the plant is usually the first resort of the railway manager when pressed for immediate money to pay bond interest. Then there are always demands for new capital for improvements necessary to be made by every railway as its traffic increases. Ordinarily bonds are sold to meet these capital charges. If, because of a lack of confidence on the part of the investing public, or a lack of credit as regards this particular company, such bonds cannot be sold, except perhaps at a great sacrifice, then the management proceed to borrow the necessary money for these capital improvements and perhaps for the then due bond interest. Usually the company must hypothecate with the bankers from whom the money is borrowed bonds either of the company itself or such as are held in its treasury and controlling subsidiary lines important to the integrity of the system, so that the banker's loan may be fully secured. If matters go from bad to worse, if it appear to the lender that the situation of the company is becoming more and more critical, so that he is beginning to doubt the real value of the collaterals held by him, he then calls for his money, if it is loaned on demand, or gives notice that he will ask for it when the same shortly matures. If the company cannot arrange to borrow the amount from some one else, and if it is confronted with the sale of all its securities at bankrupt prices, the managers may resolve to confess their own insolvency before a public confession is made by the sale of the securities held by the banker. Perhaps, just at this moment, a large amount of interest is due to bondholders. In such a case the railway managers may choose to default on the bond interest and take the money for payment to the floating-debt holders, in order to save for the company the collateral which the bankers may hold, and which may be essential to the control of parts of the system, but which would very likely go for a song if pressed for immediate sale. While, therefore, floating debts do not differ from other obligations of the company except in form, they have come to be recognized in Wall Street as a source of great danger in any period of business depression or lack of credit. If this money borrowed on demand or on short notice can be funded into bonds having years to run, the company cannot suffer through a demand upon it for the principal, but it is safe so long as the interest is promptly paid. This reasoning has led railway companies at times to adopt the plan of selling long-time bonds in order to pay off the floating debt, even though the price received should be far below par. But such a course compels the company to pay a very high rate of interest during the whole life of the bonds and is considered such bad financiering that such sales are taken in Wall Street as an acknowledgment that the company is hard pressed—with results to the credit of the corporation almost as bad as though the distress had been openly acknowledged. Under these circumstances,

" friendly " receivers are often asked for so that interest may be withheld from the bondholders and used to
take up the obligations of the company immediately
pressing, particularly in cases where a failure to meet
those obligations would entail severe losses upon the
system for all time.

The court appointing receivers thus asked for usually stipulates that debts incurred in the operation of a
road for several months shall be paid by the receivers.
At first blush it would appear that such an order entails
hardship upon the creditors of the company, yet upon
examination it will be found to be equitable. Transportation is conducted as a cash business. Travellers
and shippers are required to pay their money down
before taking their journey or receiving their property.
Since a railway must be run in the interest of the general public, and since this involves the theory that its
working expenses must be paid, it is clear that the
expenses of to-day are properly chargeable to the gross
receipts of to-day paid in cash by the patrons of the
road. But, as we have seen, in periods of distress, the
managers in order to postpone a confession of bankruptcy in the hopes that the temporary trouble may be
tided over, begin to put off payments for wages or for
coal, rails, ties, and supplies of all descriptions which
they may continue to buy, because necessary for the
continued operation of the trains. In this way, at the
date of appointment of receivers, every bankrupt road
has large arrears of wages and accounts to be made up.
As these current obligations are realy chargeable to
the receipts of the several months past, and as these
receipts have been taken to pay bond interest or for
other purposes in the interest of the bondholders, it is
proper that the prior claims for current expenses should

be made up from the first receipts of the road under the receivership. If there is any complaint to be made on the part of the bondholders, it is that the knowledge of these facts has not been brought to their attention ; but usually in such a matter the managers of the road act in good faith, in the hopes that better times may enable them to pay up the back debts and save the indirect losses to the bondholders, which a public confession of the real situation would at that time have caused.

The heavy expenses confronting the receivers at the time of their appointment are met partly from defaulted bond interest and perhaps from receivers' certificates. At first these certificates, generally made a first lien on the property, were authorized very sparingly by the courts and only in cases shown beyond dispute to be necessary. Gradually such issues were extended, until the present practice is for authorization of certificates for any purpose which the court may be led to believe is for the ultimate benefit of the road. In this way another mortgage is put ahead of the regular mortgage whose bonds, held by the public, have been supposed and declared to be a prior lien upon the road. The force of circumstances often thus impairs the rights of existing mortgages though these be drawn in strong legal language. The right to issue receivers' certificates has been, and may be, greatly abused. In one case the expense of operating greatly exceeded the receipts. The property and franchises should have been sold at once so that the first-mortgage bondholders might at least have received the value of the rails and equipment ; but the court allowed the receivers to go on running the road until the certificates issued to make up the losses amounted to more than the value of the property, the bondholders not getting a cent. Receivers' certificates should be authorized only when a careful judgment tempered by conservatism justifies their issue. As just said, the directors, at the first appearance of a decline in profits, economize in depreciation expenses, hoping for better times. If the decline continues and a receivership ensues, the passing of the property into the hands of the court is an acknowledgment of facts regarding impairment of income which are true though not before generally known. Hence the issue of receivers' certificates commercially represents the impairment of income just referred to, but which at the time was not enforced against the bondholders. Railway mortgages are not sacred because of the strong legal terms in which they are drawn, but are dependent upon success in the business of transportation, differing in this respect from real-estate mortgages which rely more upon the prosperity of the whole community. The legal doctrine of certificates is in a state of evolution, with a tendency to approximate its working to the business circumstances. Our practice of railway receiverships is thus a development of our own circumstances and a sort of compromise between the too strong language of our mortgages and the actual conditions of the business of transportation.

A receiver may decline to pay the rentals due to leased lines or the interest owing on guaranteed bonds if these lines are at the time of the receivership unprofitable, no matter how necessary to the parent company these branches may once have been. But the old contracts are still legally in force against the company, and can be thrown off only by a sale of the franchise and property to a new corporation. Such a sale sometimes would involve a forfeiture of valuable charter rights besides a long legal struggle ; and in such reorganizations committees usually try to formulate some plan which shall bring the fixed charges below the minimum profits by allotting the necessary losses among all classes of securities in proportion to their respective values to the system as a whole—a process which does not regard the liens of the mortgages so much as the worth of the lines they cover. But with plans of reorganization, the receiver properly should have nothing to do.

The legal doctrine and the practice regarding receiverships and receivership problems have, in the United States, been developed thus far largely in the affairs of railways. Railways so clearly have public duties to perform that it was inevitable that questions regarding their continued operation should require settlement. This point once settled, matters of detail about the proper working would naturally come up for adjustment in the order of their commercial evolution.

For these reasons we find the custom regarding railway receiverships much in advance of those concerning other corporations. But though these latter lag behind, there are not wanting signs that some of the problems of this character which we are trying to solve in transportation, are in the future to demand consideration in manufacturing. When factories were numerous but small and easily managed by an individual or by a firm composed of but few persons, it was not a matter of great public moment whether one or two firms failed. The demand could be easily supplied by the manufacturers still in business and perhaps the factory itself, belonging to the insolvent partners, would be re-opened and run by another firm. The case is altered already, if we have in mind the large corporations formed to do certain manufacturing on an extensive scale, and the point is likely to demand more attention in the future, when, in the probable evolution of things, the greater part of our manufactured output may be produced by a comparatively few companies having large capital, extensive plants, and the best of appliances—for to such a state of production are we slowly tending.

Already cases of the insolvency of large manufacturing companies have been before the courts. In appointing receivers, it is now customary in such instances to allow these officers of the courts to continue the business. Like railways, these large corporations cannot very well stop working. Not only are large bodies of laboring men dependent for bread upon this continued operation, but concerns throughout the country would be embarrassed if their orders, perhaps half executed, should not be completed at the appointed time.

Under our assumptions, it might not be possible for the customers of the corporation to obtain the required articles from any other source of supply, and certainly not in time to go ahead with their own plans,—plans which if not carried out might cause financial embarrassment to them also and to others. In short, the larger the company, the more complete the producing organization, the more important to the community is its continued operation. We have heard complaints from solvent companies or firms that the competition of factories in the hands of receivers was unfair to them, exactly as in the case of railways ; but the growing interdependence of trade and commerce leaves no other alternative.

This being so, the discussion just had on the com-

mercial facts underlying railway receiverships has a
bearing upon the immediate and future problems of
manufacturing or trading corporations.   This is all the
more true because these latter are now issuing mortgages after the manner of transportation companies.
In the present customs about railway receiverships and
their rapid evolution under the stress of actual conditions, and in the philosophy which seems to underlie
those customs, we may catch glimpses of the probable
experience awaiting the community if large business
corporations are to do the most of our manufacturing,
and if the managers of those companies should repeat
the financial blunders or frauds which appear in our
past railway history, or if commercial disaster should
compel a readjustment of capital.

INDEX.

A

Accountants, public, 19 ; judging of business, 20

Accounting with branch lines, 69 ; losses of branch lines, 72–74 ; charging off old deficits, 74 ; difficulty in setting forth facts, 80 ; excuse for optimism, 80 ; truth might destroy credit and chance for recovery, 80 ; general balance - sheets, 81 ; should show full details, 81, 82 ; profit and loss account, 82 ; treatment of depreciation, 83, 84 ; charging to income or capital, 82–84 ; betterments on British railways, 85 ; betterments on American railways, 85, 86 ; operating expenses, 87 ; importance of knowing cost of plant, 88 ; for small companies, 88

Accounting for mercantile corporations, 89 ; cash, meaning of, 91 ; customers' bills receivable, 92 ; indirect obligations, 93 ; customers' accounts, 94 ; merchandise, 95 ; character of goods dealt in, 96 ; table of liquidation values, 97 ; real estate, 97 ; machinery and fixtures, 97 ; merchandise in bond, 98 ; proportion of profits to sales, 99 ; estimate of liabilities and assets revalued, 99, 100 ; statements of condition, 100, 101

Accounting of railways, 102 ; income account, 103 ; general balance-sheet, 106, 137 ; capital losses through lack of credit, 107 ; explanation of assets, 107 ; explanation of liabilities, 108 ; bills payable for supplies, 108, 169 ; accrued interest, 108 ; audited vouchers, 108 ; rebates and cut-rates, 109 ; profit and loss, 109 ; details of general balance-sheet, 107–109 ; tabulated changes in general balance-sheets, 110 ; expenditures and resources in yearly statements, 111 ; losses of subsidiary companies as assets, 111 ; expenditures for capital, how gathered, 112, 113 ; increase in cost of road and equipment, 113–115 ; statement of equipment, 115 ; life of rails, 116 ; percentage of operating expenses to earnings, 117 ; examples of operating expenses, 117, 118 ; maintenance of way, 119, 169 ; maintenance of equipment, 119, 169 ; average number of passengers to train, 120 ; cost of fuel, 120 ; cost of motive power, 120 ; freight train lading, 120 ; freight cars and freight car mileage, 121, 122 ; general expenses, 122 ; table of quick assets and liabilities, 123 ; bonds in treasury, 123, 124 ; saving a railway, 124 ; income account under change